My Diary

1883

Sarah Jane S.

Table of Contents

Copyright 1984
Joan Vibert & Linda Brannock
Made & Printed in the USA

Welcome to the world of Sarah Jane. We will admit it is a fictional world. We have spent the last four months researching childhood on the Kansas prairie in the 1800's. Our fascination with the subject led us to pretending that we were little girls in that era. It was from that pretending that this book evolved. We have had so much fun that we know you will enjoy it also.

These dolls are addictive! Don't be surprised if your family becomes mildly anxious over your mental state. It is probably a valid concern when grown women are seen dressing dolls. We found that there was always one more doll we wanted to try. Eventually we had to quit to write this book.

Our family, friends, and students encouraged us with much enthusiam while this book was in process. A large debt of gratitude must go to our friend and cohort, Terry Thompson. If she had not moved to Leadville, Colorado and gotten out of our hair, this book may never have been written.

A special thanks to Jane Braverman, Gloria Hanaway and Joyce Whittier for their many hours of proof-reading. Love to Kristy for her handwriting, to Sara for her inspiration and Lindsey for her patience.

For those of you who may be interested in further reading, we would like to give you a list of the books which most inspired us:

PIONEER WOMEN by Joanna L. Stratton, A Touchstone Book published by Simon & Schuster
SMALL FOLK by Sandra Brant & Elissa Cullman, Published by E. P. Dutton
AMERICAN FOLK DOLLS by Wendy Lavitt, Alfred A. Knopf, Publisher
All of the "LITTLE HOUSE" books by Laura Ingalls Wilder, Harper & Row, Publishers

The year is 1883. Eight year old Sarah Jane lives with Ma and Pa and baby Molly in a small cabin on the ever expanding Kansas prairie. Their cabin is shared with an orange kitty named Muffie. Sarah Jane's childhood is full of hard work, but between the chores she has happy times that are filled with love and wonder. These are the times she writes about in her diary.

1

Janary 1, 1883

I got a new pencil and tablet of my very own for Christmas

FROM PA. I AM GOING TO KEEP A DIARY AND WRITE IN IT EVERY DAY. MA SAYS
THAT A DIARY IS VERY IMPORTANT TO KEEP. SHE LEFT THE ONE SHE HAD WHEN
SHE WAS A LITTLE GIRL IN OHIO WHEN WE CAME TO KANSAS. BUT SHE HAS A NEW
ONE NOW AND IT TELLS ABOUT OUR TRIP AND I GET TO READ IT WHEN I GET BIG.
I ALSO GOT SOME STICKS OF CANDY FOR CHRISTMAS AND I AM GOING TO SAVE THE
REST OF THEM FOR A REAL LONG TIME. MA MADE ME A NEW SCARF, A RED ONE.
SHE MADE MOLLY A NEW HAT AND PA MADE HER BLOCKS. IT WAS FUN.

JANARY 2 WE GOT A WHOLE LOT OF SNOW LAST NIGHT. PA COULD NOT OPEN THE
DOOR THIS MORNING. I PLAYED WITH MY PAPER DOLLS TODAY AND MA LET ME USE
SOME OF THE CHRISTMAS PAPER TO MAKE NEW CLOTHES FOR THEM. MOLLY WANTS
TO PLAY WITH MY DOLLS BUT I TOLD HER SHE WAS TOO LITTLE. BECAUSE SHE
DOES NOT KNOW HOW TO BE CAREFUL WITH THEM. SHE TORE THE FOOT ON MY BOY
DOLL, BUT I DIDN'T GET MAD. HE IS NOT MY BEST ONE.

JANARY 3 MOLLY BURNED HER FINGER ON THE STOVE TODAY. I WAS WATCHING
HER BECAUSE MA AND PA WERE OUTSIDE TO BREAK UP THE WOODPILE. SHE CRIED
A WHOLE LOT AND WANTED ME TO HOLD HER. I TOLD HER A STORY. WHEN MA CAME
IN SHE GOT OUT THE BUTTON BAG AND I PUT BUTTONS ON A STRING FOR MOLLY
TO PLAY WITH AND THAT MADE HER HAPPY. MA TOLD ME AND MOLLY A STORY ABOUT
THE REAL OLD BUTTONS. WHEN PA CAME IN HE HELPED ME WITH ARITHMETIC AND
WE DID TAKE AWAY WITH THE BUTTONS. IT WAS FUN. I LIKE SNOWY DAYS BECAUSE
PA IS IN THE HOUSE WITH US.

JANARY 4 I HATE SNOW. I WENT OUT WITH PA THIS MORNING TO FEED THE CHICKENS
THE SNOW WAS SO DEEP THAT PA HAD TO CARRY ME SOMETIMES. MY SCARF BLEW
AWAY AND PA HAD TO RUN AND GET IT. I WAS IN THE CHICKEN HOUSE ALL BY
MYSELF AND THE CHICKENS WERE PECKING AT ME AND FLAPPING THEIR WINGS.
I RAN OUTSIDE TO CALL PA. HE WAS AT THE FOOD BIN AND I COULD NOT FIND
HIM. THE WIND WAS SO LOUD AND PA COULD NOT HEAR ME. I HATE CHICKENS
TOO!

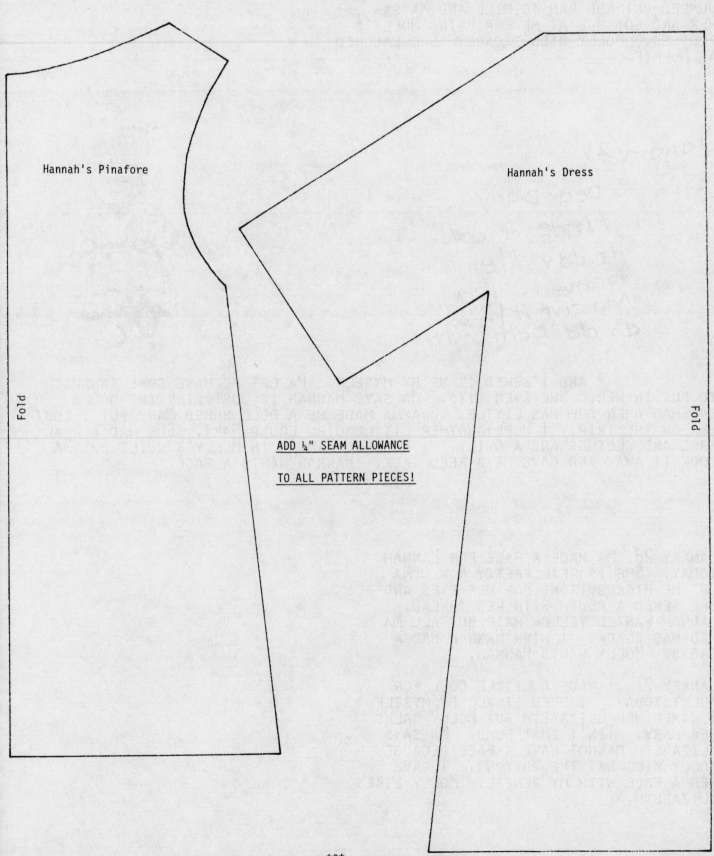

Hannah's Pinafore

Hannah's Dress

Fold

Fold

ADD ¼" SEAM ALLOWANCE

TO ALL PATTERN PIECES!

JANARY 5 MA WAS REAL MAD AT ME TODAY.
SHE WAS MAKING BREAD AND I WAS PLAYING
HOUSE WITH MUFFIE. I DRESSED HER IN
MOLLY'S NIGHTGOWN AND BONNET. SHE
LOOKED REAL CUTE. BUT SHE WOULD NOT
STAY IN THE BED I MADE FOR HER. SHE
JUMPED OUT AND RAN TO HIDE AND MA SAW
HER AND GOT MAD AT ME FOR USING MOLLY'S
CLOTHES. MOLLY DIDN'T CARE. SHE LAUGHED
AT MUFFIE.

Janary 21

Dear Diary
I made a doll
today. Her
name iz Hannah.
Ma cut it from
an old petticoat

AND I SEWED IT UP BY MYSELF. PA LET ME HAVE SOME SAWDUST
TO PUT IN HER. SHE EVEN SITS. MA SAYS HANNAH IS JUST LIKE THE DOLLS
SHE HAD WHEN SHE WAS LITTLE. GRAMMA MADE ME A DOLL NAMED MARY BUT I LOST
HER ON THE TRIP. I HOPE ANOTHER LITTLE GIRL FOUND MARY. SHE HAD A REAL
FACE AND CLOTHES AND A QUILT. I WRAPPED HANNAH IN MOLLY'S QUILT BUT MA
TOOK IT AWAY AND GAVE ME A FEED SACK. HANNAH WANTS A FACE.

JANARY 26 MA MADE A FACE FOR HANNAH
TODAY. SHE IS REAL PRETTY NOW. MA
LET ME PICK BUTTONS FOR HER EYES AND
SHE SEWED A MOUTH WITH RED THREAD.
HANNAH WANTED YELLOW HAIR BUT ALL MA
HAD WAS BLACK. I WISH HANNAH HAD A
DRESS. MOLLY WANTS HANNAH.

JANARY 27 I MADE A LITTLE DOLL FOR
MOLLY TODAY. I DREW IT ALL BY MYSELF.
I NAMED HER ELIZABETH BUT MOLLY CALLS
HER BABY. ISN'T THAT DUMB? MA SAYS
ELIZABETH CANNOT HAVE A FACE BECAUSE
MOLLY WILL EAT THE BUTTONS. I GAVE
HER A FACE WITH MY PENCIL. MOLLY LIKES
ELIZABETH.

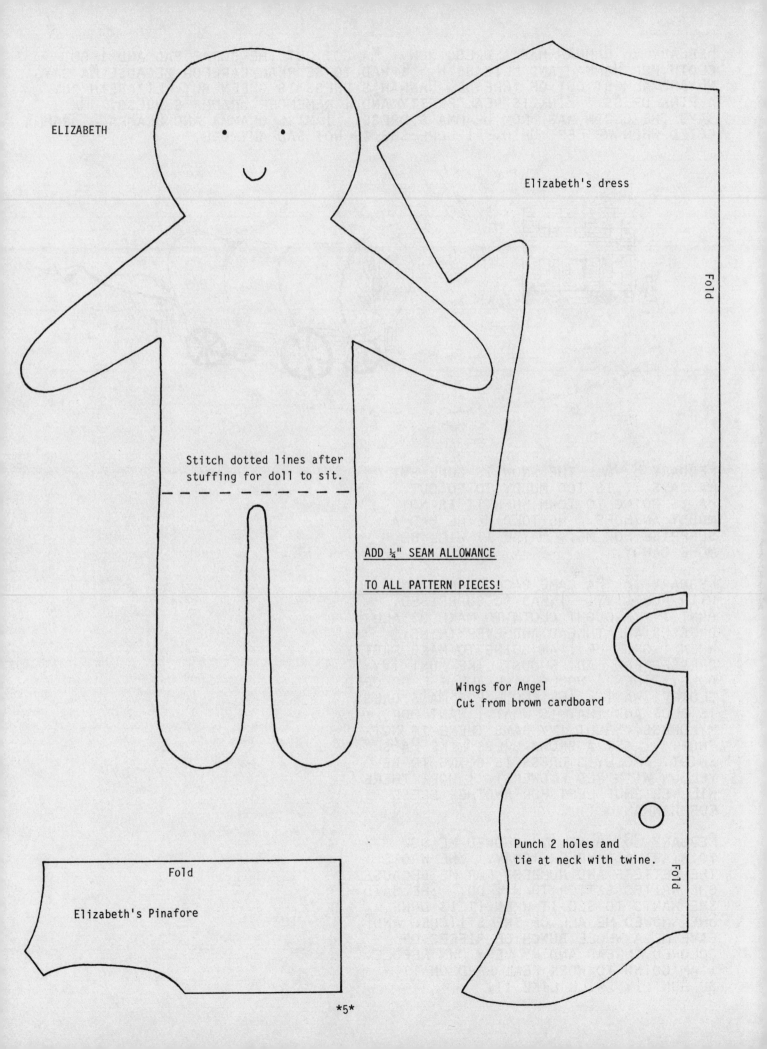

ELIZABETH

Elizabeth's dress

Fold

Stitch dotted lines after
stuffing for doll to sit.

ADD ¼" SEAM ALLOWANCE

TO ALL PATTERN PIECES!

Wings for Angel
Cut from brown cardboard

Punch 2 holes and
tie at neck with twine.

Fold

Fold

Elizabeth's Pinafore

FEBUARY 2 HANNAH HAS A DRESS NOW. MA GOT OUT THE SCRAP BAG AND I GOT
CLOTH FOR HANNAH AND ELIZABETH. I HAD TO BE REAL CAREFUL BECAUSE MA SAYS
WE ARE ALMOST OUT OF THREAD. HANNAH'S DRESS IS GREEN BUT ELIZABETH GOT
A PINK DRESS. PINK IS REAL PRETTY AND I REMEMBER GRAMMA'S DRESS. MA
SAYS THE CLOTH WAS FROM GRAMMA'S DRESS. I MISS GRAMMA AND GRAMPA. GRAMMA
CRIED WHEN WE LEFT OHIO. I HOPE SHE IS NOT SAD ANYMORE.

FEBUARY 8 ALL THE SNOW IS GONE BUT
MA SAYS IT IS TOO MUDDY TO GO OUT.
PA IS GOING TO TOWN WHEN IT IS NOT
MUDDY ANYMORE. HE TOLD ME HE HAD A
SURPRISE FOR ME. MAYBE IT WILL BE
MORE CANDY.

FEBUARY 17 PA CAME BACK FROM TOWN
WITH AUNT IVY. I WAS SO SURPRISED.
AUNT IVY BROUGHT CLOTH TO MAKE US ALL
DRESSES AND THREAD AND EVERYTHING.
WHEN I GROW UP I AM GOING TO MAKE PRETTY
DRESSES FOR LADIES JUST LIKE AUNT IVY
DOES. THEN I WOULD HAVE ALL THE COLORED
CLOTH I WANT. THE CLOTH FOR MA'S DRESS
IS BLUE AND THAT IS WHAT I WANT FOR
MY DRESS. AUNT IVY SAYS THERE IS NOT
ENUF. I GET A BROWN DRESS LIKE PA'S
SHIRT. MOLLY'S DRESS IS GOING TO BE
YELLOW WITH RED FLOWERS. I HOPE THERE
WILL BE ENUF LEFT FOR ANOTHER DRESS
FOR HANNAH.

FEBUARY 20 AUNT IVY SHOWED ME HOW
TO START A SAMPLER TODAY. SHE WROTE
THE LETTERS AND NUMBERS FOR ME BECAUSE
SHE WRITES BETTER THAN I DO. SHE SAID
SHE WANTS TO SEE IT WHEN IT IS DONE.
SHE SHOWED ME ALL OF THE STITCHES AND
GAVE ME A WHOLE BUNCH OF PIECES OF
COLORED THREAD AND MY VERY OWN NEEDLE.
I AM GOING TO WORK REAL HARD ON IT
SO AUNT IVY WILL LIKE IT.

Sarah's Sampler

Supplies
    Feed sack or Onasburg cloth about
    12 X 15 inches
    Several colors of floss
    Wood frame to fit

The sampler shown is 10½ X 12½ inches. You may either use our sampler pattern or create your own free hand version. If you have a little girl to stitch it, you have a real bonus. We have drawn Sarah's sampler as a little girl of eight might have stitched it. This gives us the advantage of not having to second-guess an eight year old.

Instructions: Transfer sampler letters to a single sheet of tracing paper. The dotted lines indicate where the letters overlap for transferring. Trace from the tracing paper onto your fabric, leaving a 1 inch border all the way around.

Stitch with 3 strands of embroidery floss using any stitches desired. We used just a combination of running stitches and back stitches. After stitching was completed, the sampler was tea-dyed. This toned down the colors of the floss. After dyeing, dry flat. Frame.

If you have a frame for which you would like to make an "antique" sampler, measure the opening and add 1 inch all the way around. Figure the number of lines required for the large and small letters, numbers and a name and age. (It might be fun to use your favorite Grandmother's name.) Indicate the lines you need with strips of masking tape. Draw on the alphabet and numbers with a water soluble pen. Don't try to make it perfect. After stitching, follow the instructions that came with the pen for removing the lines. Proceed as above.

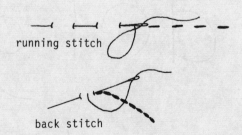

running stitch

back stitch

A B C D E

J K L M

S T U V W

c d e f g h i j k l m

v w x y z 1 2 3 4

Sarah Jane

E F G H I
N O P Q R
W X Y Z a b
l m n o p q r s t u
3 4 5 6 7 8 9 0
a n e   A g e 8

Febuary 28
    Ma and Aunt Ivy are still sewing on Ma's quilt.

THEY ARE
SEWING THE PIECES TOGETHER AND IT IS FUN TO WATCH. AUNT IVY SHOWED MA
A NEW PATTERN SHE SAW. MA SAID IT WAS REAL PRETTY BUT SHE COULD NEVER
MAKE IT BECAUSE IT WOULD TAKE SO MUCH TIME. I THINK AUNT IVY COULD MAKE
IT. I HOPE SHE NEVER EVER LEAVES.

MARCH 2 TODAY I MADE 2 MORE DOLLS
FOR HANNAH TO PLAY WITH. HANNAH LIKES
THEM BECAUSE NOW SHE HAS A FAMILY.
AUNT IVY SEWED REAL PRETTY HAIR ON
THE ONE WITH LETTERS FROM THE FEED
SACK ON IT. I NAMED HER JOSEPHINE
BECAUSE MA SAID SHE WAS LIKE A QUEEN
IN FRANCE ACROSS THE OCEAN. AUNT IVY
SAID THE OTHER DOLL SHOULD BE A BOY
SO I NAMED HIM GEORGE. HE WAS OUR
PRESIDENT. GEORGE DOESN'T HAVE ANY
HAIR BUT AUNT IVY MADE HIM A CAP FROM
MY OLD SOCK TO KEEP HIS HEAD WARM.
HE HAS PANTS LIKE PA.

MARCH 5 MRS. LOGAN AND CHARITY CAME
TODAY. MR. LOGAN AND PA MADE A NEW
FENCE. MRS. LOGAN AND MA AND AUNT
IVY SEWED ON MA'S QUILT. THE SNOW
IS GONE BUT IT IS COLD OUTSIDE. ME
AND CHARITY PLAYED UNDER THE QUILT
FRAME. WE STARTED MAKING QUILTS FOR
OUR DOLLS. CHARITY BROUGHT HER DOLL
NAMED PRISSY. SHE DIDN'T KNOW I HAD
THREE DOLLS. I THINK SHE IS JEALOUS.
MY QUILT IS NAMED FLYING GEESE. I
AM MAKING THAT ONE BECAUSE MA ONLY
GAVE ME A TRIANGLE TO USE. CHARITY
IS SUCH A SHOW OFF. SHE HAD A WHOLE
LOT OF SHAPES TO USE. THEY WERE IN
HER MA'S SEWING BASKET. SHE SAID THEY
WERE FROM HER GRAMMA IN PENNSYLVANIA.
SHE SAID HER QUILT IS NAMED FOX AND
GEESE AND IT IS HARDER THAN MINE.
I THINK SHE IS A COPY CAT. SHE DIDN'T
GET PRETTY COLORS FOR HER QUILT LIKE
ME.

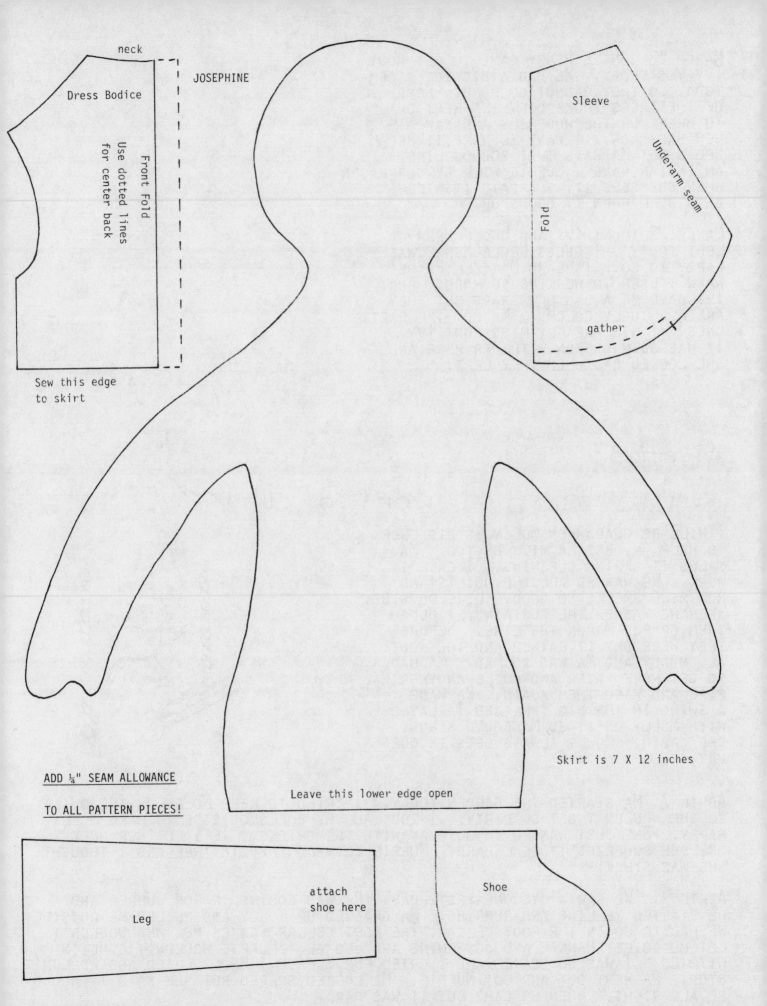

neck

JOSEPHINE

Dress Bodice

Front Fold
Use dotted lines
for center back

Sew this edge
to skirt

Sleeve

Underarm seam

Fold

gather

ADD ¼" SEAM ALLOWANCE

TO ALL PATTERN PIECES!

Skirt is 7 X 12 inches

Leave this lower edge open

Leg

attach
shoe here

Shoe

MARCH 18 UNCLE HENRY CAME TO GET AUNT
IVY YESTERDAY. WE HAD A BIG ICE STORM
TODAY SO THEY CANNOT GO HOME. SOME
OF THE TREES BROKE OFF. PA WENT OUT
TO BREAK UP THE WOODPILE AND SAW A
NEW BABY COW. I WANT TO NAME IT RED
SPOTS BUT MA SAYS THAT SOUNDS LIKE
AN INDIAN NAME. MUFFIE WILL BE SURPRISED
WHEN SHE SEES IT. PA SAID IT WILL
BE A BULL WHEN IT GROWS UP.

MARCH 22 AUNT IVY AND UNCLE HENRY
LEFT TODAY. I GUESS UNCLE HENRY WAS
HAPPY TO GO. I HEARD MA TELL PA HE
WASN'T USED TO WORKING SO HARD. AUNT
IVY GAVE ME A BAG OF SCRAPS BUT THEY
ARE REAL UGLY COLORS. MA GOT THE PRETTY
ONES. I WILL REALLY MISS AUNT IVY.
IT WAS SO MUCH FUN WITH HER HERE AND
SHE LOOKED SAD WHEN THEY LEFT.

Abril 3

ma and I worked all week.

I WILL BE GLAD WHEN MOLLY IS BIG ENUF
TO HELP. I BET MA WILL BE TOO. MA
CALLS IT SPRING CLEANING. I CALL IT
WORK. WE WASHED ALL THE QUILTS AND
NOW MINE SMELLS SO GOOD. LIKE OUTSIDE.
WHEN WE WASHED THE CURTAINS, I HUNG
THEM UP FOR MA ON THE LINE. BEFORE
THEY WERE DRY IT RAINED AND THEY GOT
ALL MUDDY AND MA WAS SO MAD. MA HAD
TO GET MORE WATER AND BUILD ANOTHER
FIRE AND WASH THEM AGAIN. PA MADE
A SWING IN THE BIG TREE AND I PLAYED
WITH MOLLY ON IT SO MA COULD SCRUB
THE CABIN. MOLLY ALWAYS GETS IN OUR
WAY.

ABRIL 7 MA STARTED THE GARDEN TODAY. I TRIED TO KEEP MOLLY ON THE QUILT
SO SHE WOULDN'T GET SO DIRTY. I TOOK ALL MY DOLLS OUTSIDE TO MAKE MOLLY
HAPPY. SHE JUST WANTED TO GO PLAY WITH THE CHICKS. IF I LET HER HOLD
ONE SHE SQUEEZES IT REAL HARD. MUFFIE CLIMBED THE BIG TREE AND I THOUGHT
SHE WAS STUCK.

ABRIL 21 WE SAW A CYCLONE YESTERDAY. PA WAS COMING IN FOR SUPPER AND
HE STARTED YELLING AND RUNNING. MA GRABBED UP MOLLY AND PULLED ME OUTSIDE.
WE HAD TO GO IN THE ROOT CELLAR. THE ROOT CELLAR SCARES ME. PA WOULDN'T
LET ME GO GET HANNAH AND JOSEPHINE AND GEORGE. MUFFIE WOULDN'T COME IN
WITH US. I WAS SO SCARED AND I CRIED FOR MUFFIE. MOLLY CRIED AND WOULDN'T
STOP. PA WENT OUT AND GOT MUFFIE. MA LOOKED SCARED BUT SHE SAID IT WOULD
BE ALL RIGHT. WHEN WE CAME OUT IT WAS DARK.

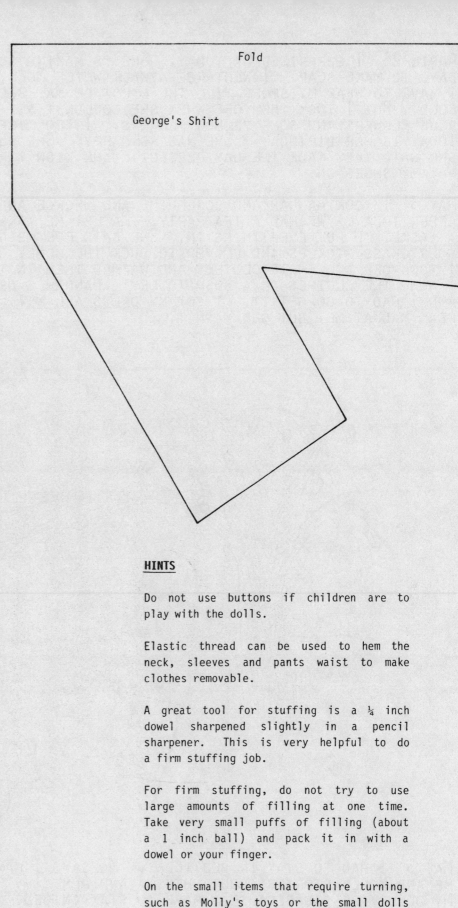

ADD ¼" SEAM ALLOWANCE

TO ALL PATTERN PIECES!

Fold

Pantaloons for Hannah

Pants for George

Use dotted lines for George's pants

HINTS

Do not use buttons if children are to play with the dolls.

Elastic thread can be used to hem the neck, sleeves and pants waist to make clothes removable.

A great tool for stuffing is a ¼ inch dowel sharpened slightly in a pencil sharpener. This is very helpful to do a firm stuffing job.

For firm stuffing, do not try to use large amounts of filling at one time. Take very small puffs of filling (about a 1 inch ball) and pack it in with a dowel or your finger.

On the small items that require turning, such as Molly's toys or the small dolls for the garland, take your time and do not try to rush it. Turn the narrow areas a little bit at a time. Sometimes it will help to pull the fabric from the outside as you are pushing from the inside.

ABRIL 26 I SURPRISED MA TODAY. SHE IS MAKING SOAP. IT TAKES LOTS OF
DAYS TO MAKE SOAP. I WENT FOR A WALK WHILE MOLLY WAS SLEEPING. MA SAYS
I HAVE TO WEAR MY SHOES TILL THE FIRST OF MAY BECAUSE THE GROUND IS STILL
COLD. BUT I TOOK THEM OFF WHEN SHE COULDN'T SEE ME. I FOUND SOME PRETTY
BLUE FLOWERS AND SOME YELLOW FLOWERS. I TOOK THEM BACK TO MA BECAUSE
TODAY IS HER BIRTHDAY. SHE WAS SO HAPPY. SHE PUT THEM ON THE TABLE AND
SHE SAID THEY MADE THE DAY PERFECT. SHE DIDN'T EVEN NOTICE I FORGOT TO
PUT MY SHOES ON.

MAY 3 I TOOK HANNAH AND JOSEPHINE AND GEORGE AND ELIZABETH DOWN TO THE
CREEK TODAY. WE HAD A TEA PARTY. MA LET ME TAKE SOME SUGAR COOKIES AND
A BASKET TO PUT EVERYTHING IN. SHE SAID FOR ME NOT TO GET WET. I PICKED
SOUR GRASS PICKLES AND CLOVER TO SUCK THE HONEY OUT. AFTER THE TEA PARTY,
I TOOK OFF ALL THEIR CLOTHES AND WASHED THEM IN THE CREEK REAL CAREFUL.
I HUNG THE CLOTHES ON A BUSH TO DRY. HANNAH'S DRESS BLEW IN THE CREEK
AND I HAD TO GO GET IT. I GOT MY DRESS ALL WET. I THOUGHT MA WOULD BE
REAL MAD AT ME, BUT SHE WASN'T.

MAY 5 I HAD TO STAY IN BED TODAY. MA SAYS I HAVE A FEVER. SHE TOLD
ME AND MOLLY STORIES ABOUT WHEN MA AND AUNT IVY WERE LITTLE GIRLS IN OHIO.
MY DOLLS ARE SAD BECAUSE I HAVE TO STAY IN BED.

MAY 7 MA SAYS I CAN GET UP TOMORROW IF I STAY IN BED TODAY AND BE GOOD.
I FINISHED MY QUILT TODAY. MA SAID I DID GOOD ON IT. I WISH ALL THE
BLUE PIECES WERE THE SAME. I SEWED IN SOME PINK TO MAKE IT LONGER. NOW
IT COVERS HANNAH AND JOSEPHINE AND GEORGE IF THEY LAY REAL CLOSE.

Shoo-fly

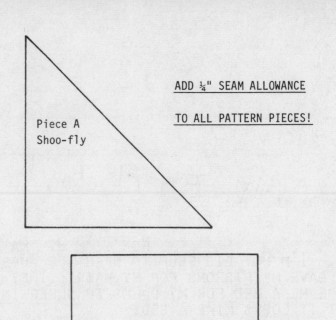

Piece A
Shoo-fly

ADD ¼" SEAM ALLOWANCE

TO ALL PATTERN PIECES!

Piece B
Shoo-fly

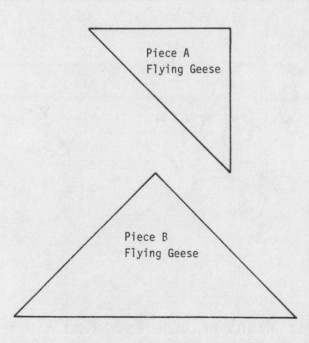

Piece A
Flying Geese

Piece B
Flying Geese

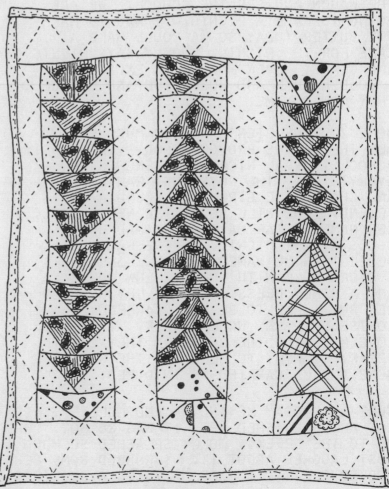

Flying Geese

May 15
My Birthday!

        NOW I AM 9. PA SAYS HIS LITTLE GIRL IS GROWING
UP. I'M NOT BIG ENUF TO OPEN THE CUPBOARD YET. I HAD A NICE BIRTHDAY.
MA GAVE ME RIBBONS FOR MY HAIR. THEY ARE ALL MY FAVORITE COLORS. PA
MADE ME A BED FOR MY DOLLS TO SLEEP IN. IT WAS A BOX WE TOOK FROM OHIO,
BUT IT LOOKS LIKE A BED.

JUNE 3 MR. TURNER CAME TODAY TO TALK
TO PA. PA TOLD MA AT SUPPER THAT THERE
WILL BE A NEW SCHOOL. PA AND MR. TURNER
AND SOME OTHER MEN ARE GOING TO BUILD
IT. MA SAYS IT WILL BE CLOSE ENUF
FOR ME TO WALK TO. I HOPE THE TEACHER
IS NICE.

JUNE 18 PA WENT TO BUILD THE SCHOOL
TODAY. MA SAID TOMORROW WE COULD TAKE
THE WAGON AND SEE THE SCHOOL. WE ARE
GOING TO HAVE A PICNIC. I HAD TO MAKE
THE BUTTER TODAY SO MA COULD MAKE A
CAKE FOR THE PICNIC. MOLLY SAYS NICNIC
AND CLAPS. EVEN MUFFIE IS EXCITED.
I TOLD HANNAH AND JOSEPHINE AND GEORGE
THEY COULD COME.

JUNE 20 THE PICNIC WAS SO MUCH FUN.
ALL THE LADIES BROUGHT FOOD. THE NEW
SCHOOL IS REAL NICE WITH BENCHES AND
EVERYTHING. THE BOYS JUST RAN AROUND
AND CHASED THE GIRLS. I FOUND A NEW
FRIEND. SHE WILL BE AT THE NEW SCHOOL.
HER NAME IS MARTHA AND SHE HAD HER
DOLLS AT THE PICNIC. THERE WAS A GIRL
OLDER THAN ME NAMED LOUISE. SHE HAD
A STORE DOLL WITH LONG YELLOW CURLS
AND A FANCY DRESS. LOUISE LET ME HOLD
HER BUT I HAD TO BE REAL CAREFUL BECAUSE
LOUISE SAID SHE WOULD BREAK. I STILL
LOVE MY DOLLS THE BEST AND THEY CAN'T
BREAK. I WENT TO SLEEP ON THE WAY
HOME AND PA CARRIED ME INTO BED.

JUNE 25 TODAY ME AND MA AND MOLLY PICKED ALL KINDS OF BERRIES. MOLLY
GOT ALL SCRATCHED UP. IT WAS SO HOT. WHEN WE WERE DONE PICKING, MA TOOK
US TO THE CREEK. MOLLY SPLASHED SO MUCH THAT MA GOT ALL WET. BUT SHE
JUST LAUGHED ABOUT IT. I RUBBED SOME BERRIES ON MY LIPS AND MA SAID I
LOOKED FUNNY. I HOPE MA MAKES A BERRIE PIE.

DOLL QUILTS

Flying Geese 15" x 18"
Shoo-Fly 12" x 18"

Supplies
Various scraps and strips of at least 3 different prints for the quilt top. More prints are better.
18" x 24" piece of fabric for backing.
15½" x 18½" piece of very flat batting or flannel.

These doll quilts should be quite flat. For this reason a piece of flannel would be very nice. Cotton Classic® by Fairfield will make it flat. Or you can pull apart a piece of traditional quilt batting by Mountain Mist. This separates nicely into two thinner pieces.

Instructions

Transfer the pattern pieces to template material. Trace around the templates on the wrong side of the fabric. Cut out, leaving ¼" seam allowances. Sew with right sides together, using a running stitch. Follow specific instructions and drawings for assembling each individual quilt.

To finish the quilts, cut batting the same size as the assembled quilt top. Cut the backing fabric one inch bigger all the way around. Pin all three layers together. Do not use a hoop! Quilt as desired or follow the suggested quilting lines in the drawings. Do not draw the lines onto the quilt. This is the fun part! No need to worry about the size of your stitches.

Bind the quilt by bringing the backing over the raw edge. Turn under about ½" and sew with a running stitch.

Flying Geese

Assemble each block by sewing two "A" pieces to one "B" piece. Sew blocks together in long strips. Sew the sashing, (about 2½" wide) to the strips. Don't cut the length of the sashing until after it is sewn to the strips. If you are making this as a primitive, the measurement will vary from strip to strip. Sew sashing to the outside edges, (about 1½" wide). Sew sashing to the top and bottom edges, (about 2").

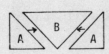
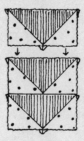

Shoo-Fly

Assemble each block by sewing four dark and light "A" triangles together. Sew these to "B" squares in rows. Sew the rows together as shown. Sew the blocks together as in the drawing.

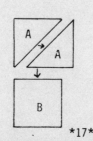
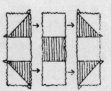

17

JUNE 26 MA MADE JAM TODAY. IT WAS
HOT IN THE CABIN AND ME AND MOLLY AND
MUFFIE PLAYED UNDER THE BIG TREE.
I MADE NECKLACES FOR ME AND MOLLY WITH
THE BERRIES. BUT MOLLY JUST WANTED
TO EAT HER NECKLACE. I USED SOME BERRIES
TO MAKE PRETTY RED LIPS ON GEORGE.
NOW HE LOOKS BETTER. WE ATE SUPPER
OUTSIDE AND MA HAD A BERRIE PIE. PA
SAID IT WAS THE BEST HE EVER HAD.

JULY 2 WE ARE ALL GOING TO TOWN FOR
INDEPENDENCE DAY. WE GET TO SLEEP
AT AUNT IVY AND UNCLE HENRY'S. MA
IS DOING LOTS OF BAKING TO GET READY
FOR THE BIG PICNIC IN TOWN. EVERYTHING
SMELLS GOOD. I HAD TO GIVE MOLLY A
BATH BUT MA WASHED OUR HAIR AND SHE
PUT MY HAIR IN RAGS. TOMORROW I WILL
HAVE BEAUTIFUL CURLS.

JULY 3 AUNT IVY IS GOING TO LET ME
AND MOLLY SLEEP OUT ON THE PORCH ON
A REAL FEATHER BED. I CAN'T WAIT FOR
TOMORROW. I CAN WRITE ALL ABOUT THE
PICNIC BECAUSE AUNT IVY GAVE ME SOME
OF HER PRETTY BLUE PAPER TO WRITE ON.

Luly 5

The picnic was real fun. We.

WENT TO CHURCH. THEN THERE WAS A REAL
LONG SPEECH BUT MA LET ME GO PLAY HIDE
AND SEEK WITH THE OTHERS. I GOT TO
BE IN THE PARADE. PA BOUGHT ME A FLAG
TO WAVE. AFTER DINNER THERE WERE RACES
AND PA AND UNCLE HENRY WON THE 3 LEGGED
RACE. THEY WERE SO FUNNY. EVERYONE
WAS FALLING DOWN. THE FIREWORKS WERE
REAL PRETTY BUT THEY SCARED MOLLY. WHEN
THE FIDDLE PLAYER CAME PA DANCED WITH
MA. I NEVER SAW THEM DANCE BEFORE.
I DANCED WITH UNCLE HENRY. THEN JUST
THE GIRLS DANCED TOGETHER. I CAN'T
REMEMBER COMING BACK TO THE HOUSE.
MA AND PA AND MOLLY WENT HOME TODAY
AND I GET TO STAY FOR A WHOLE WEEK
BY MYSELF.

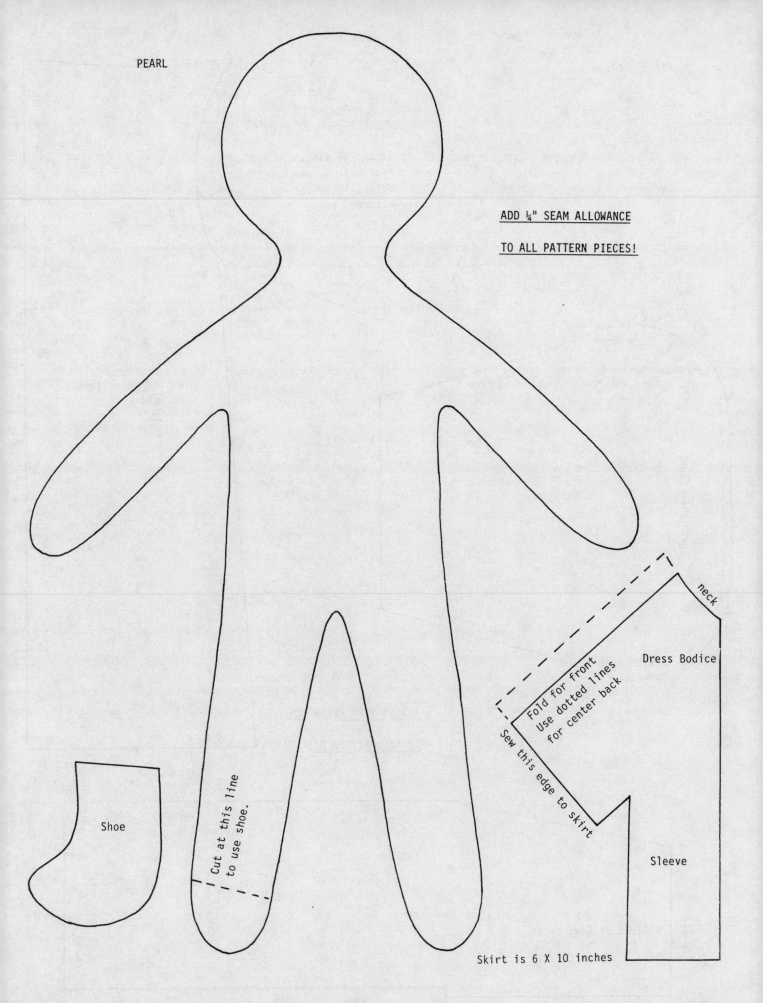

PEARL

ADD ¼" SEAM ALLOWANCE

TO ALL PATTERN PIECES!

neck

Dress Bodice

Fold for front
Use dotted lines
for center back

Sew this edge to skirt

Sleeve

Shoe

Cut at this line
to use shoe.

Skirt is 6 X 10 inches

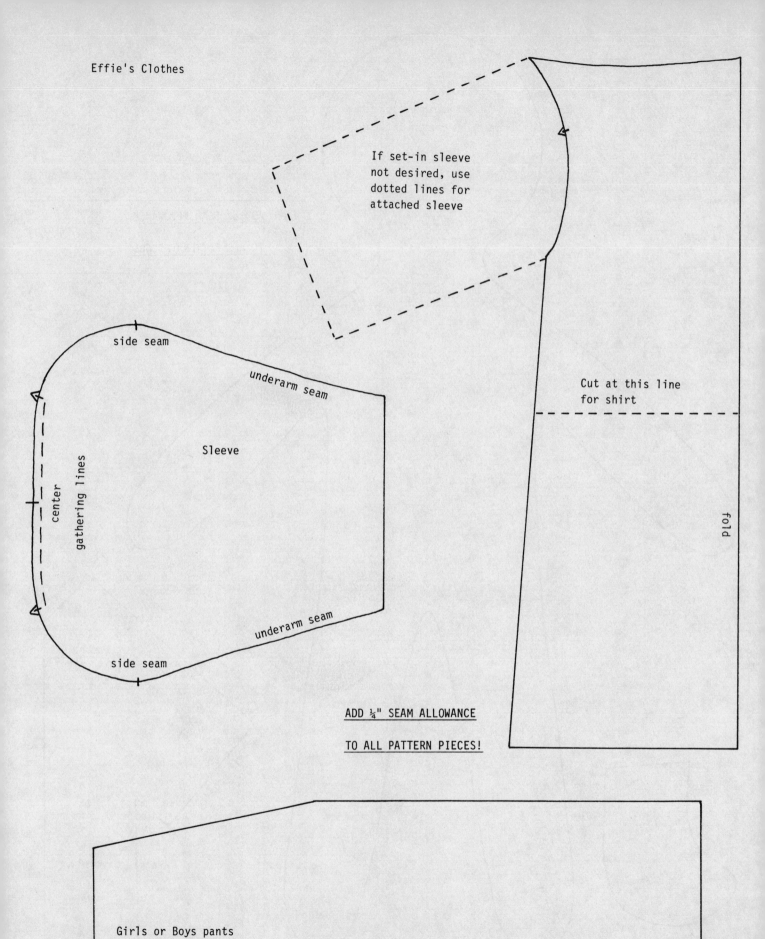

Effie's Clothes

If set-in sleeve
not desired, use
dotted lines for
attached sleeve

side seam

underarm seam

center gathering lines

Sleeve

side seam

underarm seam

Cut at this line
for shirt

fold

ADD ¼" SEAM ALLOWANCE

TO ALL PATTERN PIECES!

Girls or Boys pants

fold

20

EFFIE

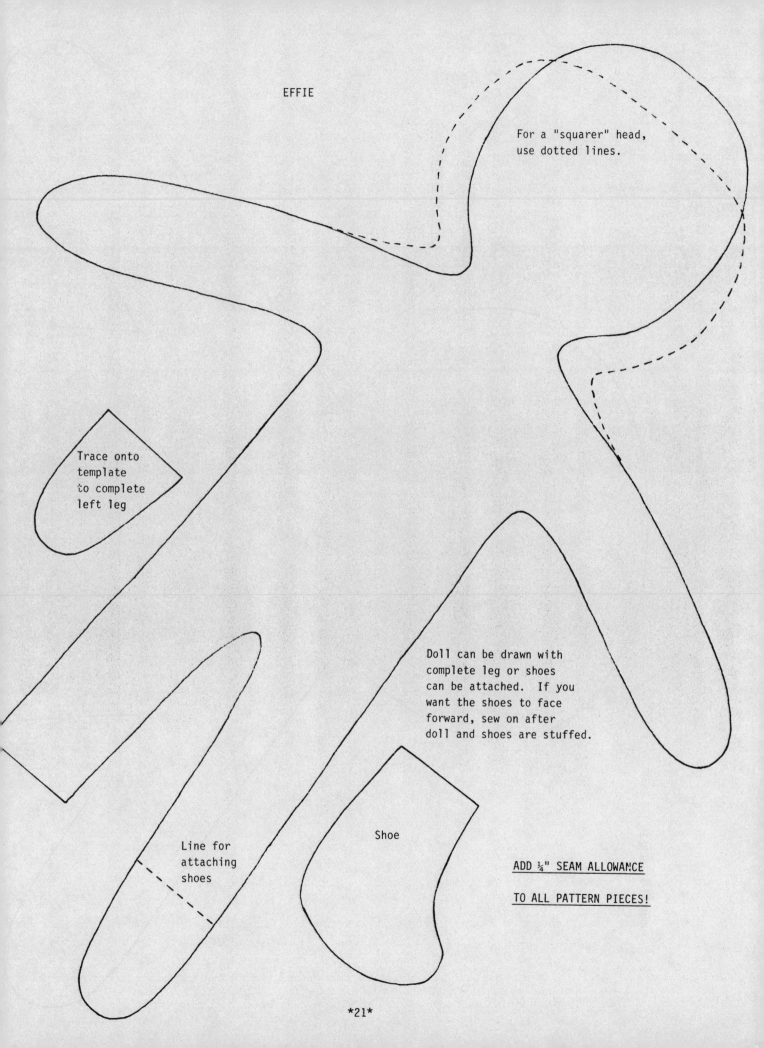

For a "squarer" head,
use dotted lines.

Trace onto
template
to complete
left leg

Doll can be drawn with
complete leg or shoes
can be attached. If you
want the shoes to face
forward, sew on after
doll and shoes are stuffed.

Line for
attaching
shoes

Shoe

ADD ¼" SEAM ALLOWANCE

TO ALL PATTERN PIECES!

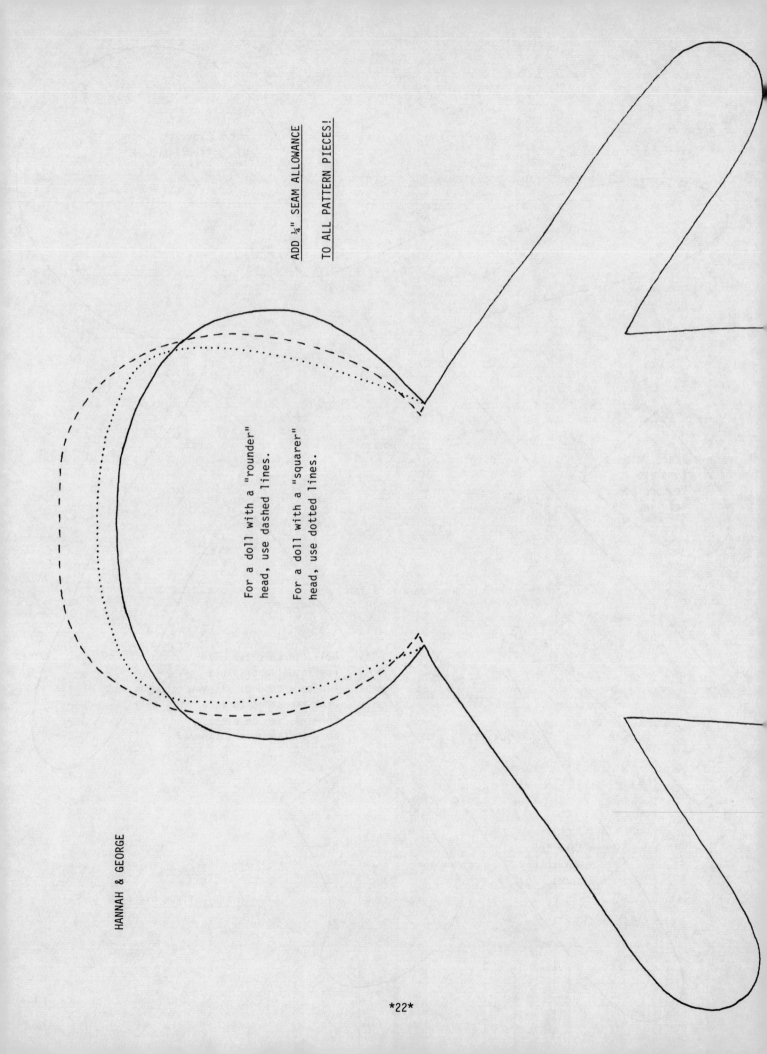

ADD ½" SEAM ALLOWANCE

TO ALL PATTERN PIECES!

For a doll with a "rounder" head, use dashed lines.

For a doll with a "squarer" head, use dotted lines.

HANNAH & GEORGE

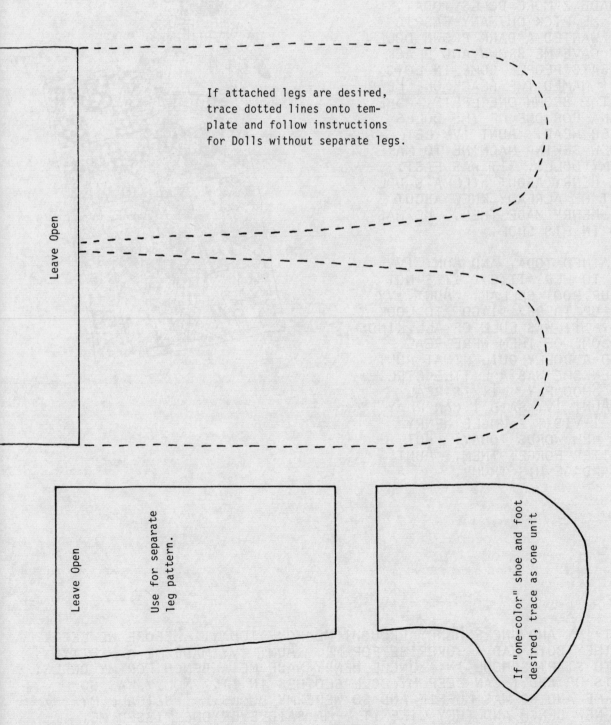

If attached legs are desired,
trace dotted lines onto template and follow instructions
for Dolls without separate legs.

Leave Open

Leave Open

Use for separate
leg pattern.

If "one-color" shoe and foot
desired, trace as one unit

JULY 6 I HAD WATERMELON TODAY. IT
TASTED SO GOOD. MRS. IRVIN HAD A TEA
TODAY AND ME AND AUNT IVY WENT. MRS.
IRVIN HAS A GIRL MY AGE NAMED STELLA.
STELLA HAS HER OWN BEDROOM. SHE HAS
A BED AND A BENCH AND CUPBOARD FOR
HER DOLLS. SHE HAS MORE DOLLS THAN
I HAVE EVER SEEN BEFORE. WE GOT TO
DRESS UP WITH HATS AND FANCY DRESSES
AND GLOVES AND PLAY MOMMY WITH HER
DOLLS. I WISH MY DOLLS WERE AT AUNT
IVY'S WITH ME. WHEN WE WERE WALKING
HOME I SAW A LADY WHO WAS DARK BROWN.

JULY 8 WE MADE 2 MORE DOLLS TODAY.
AUNT IVY LET ME PICK OUT ANY FABRIC
I WANTED. I WANTED A DARK BROWN DOLL
AND AUNT IVY GAVE ME BROWN AND BLACK
CLOTH. SHE SAYS PEOPLE COME IN LOTS
OF COLORS. I NAMED THE BLACK ONE PEARL
AND I NAMED THE BROWN ONE EFFIE. SHE
MADE A BANDANA FOR ONE OF THE DOLLS
TO WEAR ON HER HEAD. AUNT IVY LET
ME USE HER NEW SEWING MACHINE TO MAKE
DRESSES FOR MY DOLLS. IT WAS FAST.
I TOLD UNCLE HENRY ABOUT STELLA'S DOLL
FURNITURE BUT HE ALREADY KNEW ABOUT
THEM. UNCLE HENRY MADE THEM. HE HAS
LOTS OF WOOD IN HIS SHOP.

JULY 9 IT RAINED TODAY AND AUNT IVY
LET ME GO UP TO HER ATTIC. IT'S NOT
SCARY LIKE OUR ROOT CELLAR. AUNT IVY
STORES STUFF UP THERE. I GOT TO LOOK
IN HER TRUNK. IT WAS FULL OF ALL KINDS
OF THINGS. SOME OF THEM WERE REAL
OLD. I FOUND A DOLLY QUILT THAT AUNT
IVY SEWED WHEN SHE WAS A LITTLE GIRL.
IT IS CALLED SHOO-FLY. IT IS REAL
BEAUTIFUL. AUNT IVY SAID I CAN PLAY
WITH IT WHEN I VISIT. UNCLE HENRY
LEARNED ME 2 NEW WORDS TODAY. BUT
HE SAID I BETTER FORGET THEM. AUNT
IVY HAD TO BANDAGE HIS THUMB.

JULY 12 AUNT IVY AND UNCLE HENRY BROUGHT ME HOME TODAY. BEFORE WE LEFT
THEIR HOUSE THEY BOTH HAD A SURPRISE FOR ME. AUNT IVY MADE ME A PRETTY
GREEN DRESS TO START SCHOOL IN. UNCLE HENRY MADE ME A BENCH FOR MY DOLLS.
THE SEAT LIFTS UP AND I CAN KEEP MY DOLL CLOTHES IN IT. MOLLY WAS SO
HAPPY TO SEE ME AND SO WAS MUFFIE AND SO WERE MY DOLLS. I SET ALL MY
DOLLS ON THE NEW BENCH AND THEY LIKE IT. MA SAID EVERYONE MISSED ME.

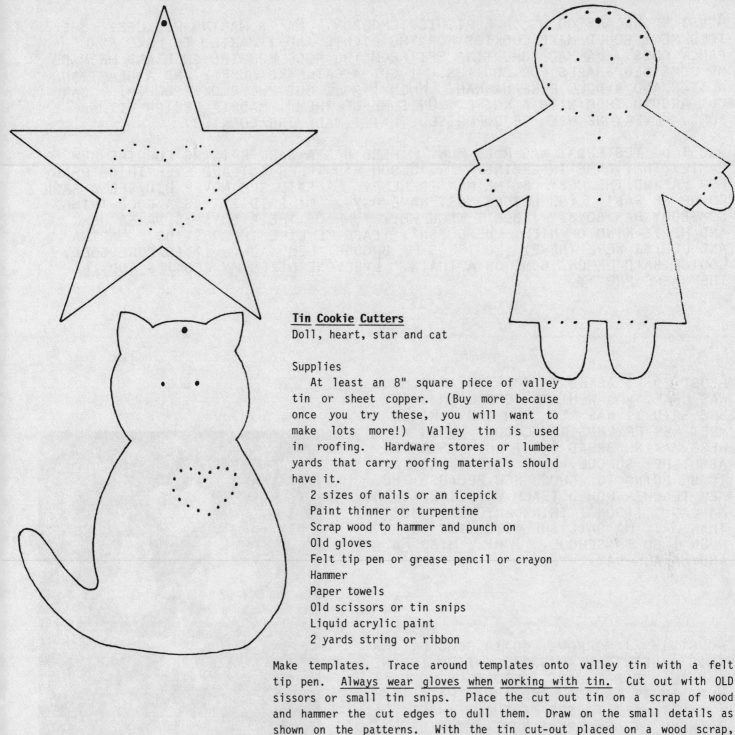

Tin Cookie Cutters
Doll, heart, star and cat

Supplies

At least an 8" square piece of valley tin or sheet copper. (Buy more because once you try these, you will want to make lots more!) Valley tin is used in roofing. Hardware stores or lumber yards that carry roofing materials should have it.

2 sizes of nails or an icepick
Paint thinner or turpentine
Scrap wood to hammer and punch on
Old gloves
Felt tip pen or grease pencil or crayon
Hammer
Paper towels
Old scissors or tin snips
Liquid acrylic paint
2 yards string or ribbon

Make templates. Trace around templates onto valley tin with a felt tip pen. Always wear gloves when working with tin. Cut out with OLD sissors or small tin snips. Place the cut out tin on a scrap of wood and hammer the cut edges to dull them. Draw on the small details as shown on the patterns. With the tin cut-out placed on a wood scrap, punch tin with a very small nail and a hammer, punching around the design. Punch a larger hole to hang them by. After punching the tin, turn over and hammer holes to dull them. Wipe the protective covering off of the tin with paint thinner.

The brightness of the tin may bother some of you. We like to hang them on our Christmas trees and for this they need to be shiny. If you prefer a dull finish, you can brush on a small amount of liquid artist's acrylic paint and wipe it right off with a paper towel. The best colors to use for this are dark (black, green or indigo). They can also be rubbed with scouring powder to remove the bright finish.

Bring both ends of a 12 X 18 inch piece of string or ribbon through the large hole punched at the top, drawing it through from the back. Tie in a bow on the front, leaving a loop on the back for hanging.

AGUST 4 WE ARE GOING ON A PICNIC TOMORROW. MA IS MAKING PICKLES. SHE
TOLD ME I COULD MAKE COOKIES FOR THE PICNIC AND I WANTED TO MAKE REAL
FANCY ONES. PA HAD SOME TIN LEFT FROM THE ROOF FOR THE SHED AND HE MADE
ME SOME NEW SHAPES FOR COOKIES. I GOT A CAT LIKE MUFFIE AND A HEART AND
A STAR AND A DOLL LIKE HANNAH. WHEN I ROLL OUT THE COOKIE DOUGH, I CAN
CUT AROUND THEM WITH A KNIFE. ON SOME OF THEM I MADE A DESIGN WITH A
FORK. EVERYONE WILL BE SURPRISED THAT I MADE THE COOKIES.

AGUST 5 YESTERDAY WAS REAL FUN. THERE WAS A BARN RAISING FOR THE NEW
FAMILY THAT CAME IN SPRING. MR. OLSON HAD TREES CUT AND EVERYTHING READY
FOR PA AND THE REST OF THE MEN TO HELP. MA SAID SHE NEVER DID SEE A BARN
GO UP SO FAST. THE OLSONS JUST HAVE BOYS. MA SAID IT WAS A GOOD THING
SOMEBODY HAS BOYS. I DON'T KNOW WHY. ONE OF THEIR BOYS IS NAMED JOHN
AND HE IS KIND OF NICE. HE DOESN'T TEASE ME LIKE THE REST DO. MARTHA
AND LOUISE WERE THERE. LOUISE'S MA BROUGHT LEMONADE. IT IS REAL GOOD.
LOUISE SAID LEMONS COME ON A TRAIN. EVERYONE LIKED MY COOKIES AND THOUGHT
THEY WERE PRETTY.

AGUST 13 I ASKED MA TODAY WHAT SCHOOL
WAS LIKE. MA WENT TO SCHOOL IN OHIO.
SHE SAID IT WAS REAL FUN AND I WOULD
MEET NEW FRIENDS AT SCHOOL. WHEN WE
WERE MAKING BREAD SHE TOLD ME STORIES
ABOUT HER SCHOOL. SHE SAID I WAS LUCKY
TO BE GOING TO SCHOOL NOW BECAUSE THE
NEW TEACHER WOULD TEACH US BETTER THAN
MA CAN. I DON'T THINK ANYONE IS BETTER
THAN MA. MA SAID SHE WILL MISS ME
WHEN I GO TO SCHOOL. I WILL MISS MA
AND PA ALL DAY.

AGUST 19 TOMORROW I GO TO SCHOOL. MA
SAID I GET TO WEAR BRAIDS WITH RIBBONS.
I REALLY DON'T WANT TO GO TO SCHOOL.
WHAT IF IT IS TOO HARD AND I HATE IT?
I CAN'T WAIT TO SEE MARTHA. I GET
TO WEAR MY NEW DRESS AUNT IVY MADE.
I HOPE THE TEACHER ISN'T MEAN.

AGUST 20 SCHOOL IS FUN. OUR TEACHER
IS NAMED MISS MCGEE AND SHE IS REAL
PRETTY. I THINK SHE IS NICE. THERE
ARE 12 OF US. MA LET ME TAKE HER SPELLER
WITH ME. MISS MCGEE PUT CHARITY AND
MARTHA ON MY BENCH TO SHARE MY BOOK.
MARTHA HAD A READER. PA GAVE ME A
BUCKET TO CARRY MY LUNCH. WE TOOK
OUR LUNCH OUTSIDE AND IT WAS LIKE A
PICNIC. WE TRADED FOOD. THE BOYS
RAN AROUND AND YELLED AND MISS MCGEE
GOT MAD AT THEM. I LIKE SCHOOL.

Dried Apple Wreath

Supplies
  2 lbs small apples
  Wire coat hanger or thinner wire
  Paper towels
  3 cookie sheets

Remove stem from apples. Slice apples, leaving core in, 1/8 - 3/16 inch thick. Lay the apple slices on a cookie sheet. Place in oven on the lowest setting for one hour. Turn apples over and bake for another hour. Turn again and leave in oven for 4 more hours, or until completely dry.

Remove the top of the coat hanger. Shape the wire into a heart using the drawing as a guide. Leave the point at the bottom open. You will need 1 inch extra wire on each side to form a hook after the apples are strung. String the apples, through the center, onto the wire. When all but 1½ inch of the wire at each end has been strung, form a hook in each end of the wire with pliers, see drawing. Hook wires together. Hang with narrow ribbon or a piece of twine. Tie each end of the string to the wire at the point shown on the drawing.

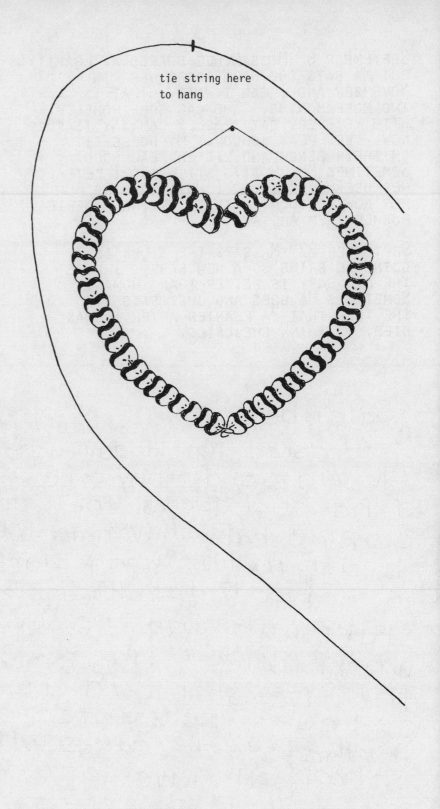

tie string here
to hang

Folkart Sugar Cookies
Makes 5½ dozen

2 egg yolks
½ cup sugar
1 cup unsalted butter, soft
1 cup sugar
2 egg whites
1 teaspoon baking soda
1 teaspoon cream of tartar
¼ teaspoon salt
1 teaspoon vanilla
3½ cups all-purpose flour
Colored sugar

1. Beat egg yolks and ½ cup sugar until thick; reserve.
2. Cream butter and 1 cup sugar until light and fluffy; beat in egg whites (batter may have a curdled look). Mix in egg yolk mixture, baking soda, cream of tartar, salt and vanilla; mix in flour gradually. Cover and refrigerate at least 1 hour.
3. Heat oven to 375 degrees. Roll out dough ¼ inch thick on lightly floured board and cut into desired shapes; place on greased baking sheets. Sprinkle cookies with colored sugar. Or roll into 1 inch balls and place on cookie sheet and press with bottom of glass dipped in colored sugar. Bake until very light brown. 8 to 10 minutes.

SEPTEMBER 6 MISS MCGEE BOARDS AT CHARITY'S
BUT MA SAYS SHE WILL BOARD HERE IN
NOVEMBER AND I CAN'T WAIT. THAT IS
TWO MORE MONTHS. SHE CAN COME HOME
WITH ME EVERY DAY. MOLLY CAN SAY TEACHER
NOW. WE PLAY SCHOOL. MY DOLLS SIT
ON THEIR BENCH AND LISTEN REAL GOOD.
SOMETIMES MOLLY SITS STILL AND I LET
HER USE MY PENCIL. I WAS TEACHING
HER HOW TO COUNT WITH STICKS AND MUFFIE
PUSHED THEM ALL AWAY.

SEPTEMBER 22 MA SAYS THE STORK IS
GOING TO BRING US A NEW BABY. I HOPE
THE NEW BABY IS BETTER THAN THOMAS.
SOMETIMES MA GOES AND JUST SITS BY
THE TREE THAT PA PLANTED AFTER THOMAS
DIED. I THINK SHE CRIES.

Setember 28
   I asked Ma today what a stork looked
like. Ma said they are even bigger than
a hawk. I guess they have to be big to
carry a baby. I wonder if they ever drop
babies in the wrong place. I might have
to go look for the new baby. I better
start watching the sky. It was night
when Molly came so I couldn't see
the the stork. Pa cried when Molly came
so I guess he wanted a boy baby. What
if the stork comes when I'm at
school? I'll have to run home.

OCTOBER 4 IT RAINED WHEN I WAS GOING TO SCHOOL THIS MORNING AND I GOT
REAL WET. MISS MCGEE PUT A FIRE IN THE STOVE AND WE DRIED OUR SHOES.
THE ROOM SMELLED AWFUL. WHEN OUR SHOES WERE DRY MISS MCGEE MADE A SURPRISE
FOR US BECAUSE WE HAD TO STAY IN. SHE MADE POPCORN. WE ATE SOME AT LUNCH.
THEN WE MADE PASTE AND PASTED THE POPCORN ON PAPER TO MAKE A WREATH.
MISS MCGEE SAID THE WREATHS ARE PRETTY IN A WINDOW AND SHE GAVE US RED
STRING TO HANG THEM UP. MA PUT MINE ON THE DOOR.

Spice Ornaments

Squeeze ½ cup applesauce in muslin to remove as much moisture as possible. Scrape applesauce into bowl and add cinnamon a teaspoon at a time. Mixture will be very stiff. Should take about 9 teaspoons. Roll out ¼ inch thick between 2 layers of wax paper. Lay on tin ornaments (punched holes toward dough) Cut around tin with a pointed knife. Leave tin in place and remove all excess dough with knife point. Remove tin by sliding knife point between tin and dough. Make hole in top of ornament for hanging. It may help to tear the wax paper between cut-outs, so you can pick each up individually. Remove wax paper from the back of the cut-out.

Place on wax paper on a cookie sheet. Set oven for lowest possible temperature (warm usually). Place in oven. Turn every 30 minutes. Bake until very dry. Takes somewhere between 2 - 4 hours depending on thickness. They do not have to bake in the oven. They can be allowed to dry on the cookie sheet. Turn daily. They should be dry in about a week depending on humidity and thickness.

Thread hole with narrow ribbon or string and tie in a bow.

The excess dough can be re-rolled and cut or you can shape it with your fingers. We like to make little one inch hearts. Poke a hole for hanging and proceed as above. These are cute in a basket or tied on a grapevine wreath.

*NOTE - Nutmeg can be substituted for the cinnamon. These are not to be eaten!

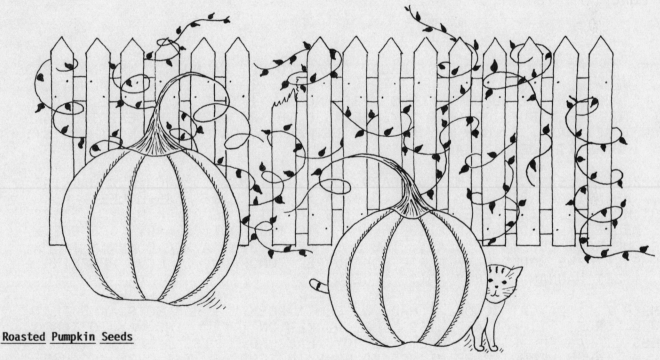

Roasted Pumpkin Seeds

2 cups seeds
1 T oil
½ t salt

Place seeds in a bowl of water as soon as removed from pumpkin. Rub off any fiber remaining. Drain in sieve and rinse. Dry on paper towels. Spread on a cookie sheet that is oiled. Toss seeds to coat. Roast in 350 degree oven for 20 minutes, tossing every 7 - 8 minutes, until golden. Remove from over and sprinkle with salt. Toss. Store in air-tight container.

OCTOBER 13   ME AND MA MADE APPLESAUCE TODAY.   I HELPED HER CORE APPLES.
WHEN SHE STARTED THE BIG FIRE OUTSIDE, I HAD TO KEEP MOLLY AWAY.   I LET
HER PLAY WITH JOSEPHINE AND GEORGE.   SHE DIDN'T LIKE THE HAT ON GEORGE
AND WANTED IT OFF.   SHE TOOK THE BANDANA OFF OF PEARL SO I TOOK THE DOLLS
INSIDE.   MA GAVE ME SOME LITTLE APPLES TO CUT FOR DRYING.   I PUT SOME
OF THEM ON A PIECE OF WIRE AND IT LOOKS LIKE A WREATH.   MA SAID I COULD
MAKE ONE FOR MISS MCGEE.

OCTOBER 14   I WISH WE HAD MORE CINNAMON.
WHEN MA AND ME WERE PUTTING UP THE
APPLESAUCE SHE TOLD ME ABOUT THE SPICE
BALLS THEY USED TO MAKE IN OHIO.   MA
SAID THEY GOT CINNAMON FROM THE PEDDLER
AND SHE ALWAYS LIKED IT WHEN SHE AND
GRAMMA MADE THEM BECAUSE THEY SMELLED
SO GOOD.   MA MIXED UP A LITTLE BIT
AND LET ME ROLL THEM OUT AND CUT THEM
WITH MY COOKIE CUTTERS.   I POKED A
HOLE IN THEM WITH MY NEEDLE AND PUT
SOME STRING IN THEM.   MA SAID WE CAN
HANG THEM ON OUR CHRISTMAS TREE.   THAT
IS A LONG TIME TO WAIT.

OCTOBER 27   ME AND MA TOOK THE WAGON TODAY TO GET WALNUTS.   WE GOT 3 BAGS
FULL.   WE WILL HAVE LOTS OF NUTS THIS WINTER.   I HATE TO PICK WALNUTS.
WHEN WE WERE IN THE WOODS I FOUND PERSIMMONS.   I TOLD MA AND SHE SAID
IT WAS TOO EARLY BUT I PICKED SOME BECAUSE THE RACOONS WILL EAT THEM AND
WE WON'T GET ANY.   I KNOW WHY MA SAID IT WAS TOO EARLY.   MY MOUTH IS STILL
DRY.   I HOPE IT DOESN'T LAST FOREVER.

NOVEMBER 5   MISS MCGEE CAME TO BOARD TODAY.   IT WAS SO MUCH FUN WALKING
HOME.   WHEN I GET BIG I AM GOING TO BE A TEACHER LIKE MISS MCGEE.   WHEN
WE GOT HOME MA SAID THERE WAS STILL TIME TO GET SOME PUMPKINS IN.   MISS
MCGEE HELPED ME AND SHE CARRIED THE BAGS TO THE ROOT CELLAR.   SHE DOESN'T
THINK THE ROOT CELLAR IS SCARY LIKE ME.   WE BROUGHT A BIG PUMPKIN TO MA
AND SHE SAID WE WOULD HAVE A PIE FOR SUPPER TOMORROW.   I LOVE PUMPKIN
PIE.   I LET HANNAH SLEEP BY MISS MCGEE.

NOVEMBER 7   TODAY AT SCHOOL I HAD TO TELL A POEM.   I WAS SO SCARED THAT
I WOULD FORGET IT.   ME AND MISS MCGEE WORKED ON IT ALL THE WAY TO SCHOOL.
I GUESS IT WAS ALL RIGHT.   ONLY THE BOYS LAUGHED.   MISS MCGEE GOT MAD
AT THEM.   WHEN WE GOT HOME WE COOKED PUMPKIN SEEDS IN THE OVEN BECAUSE
MISS MCGEE SAID THAT WAS HER FAVORITE PART OF THE PUMPKIN.

NOVEMBER 16   TODAY WAS THE LAST DAY
OF SCHOOL FOR THIS TERM.   I WISH IT
COULD GO ON BUT MISS MCGEE SAID IT
WAS TOO COLD TO WALK SO FAR.   I AM
GOING TO WORK REAL HARD ON MY STUDIES.
I WILL BE REAL SMART WHEN THE SPRING
TERM COMES.   I GUESS MISS MCGEE IS
HAPPY TO GO HOME WITH HER FAMILY.
NEXT WEEK IS THANKSGIVING.   I CAN'T
WAIT.

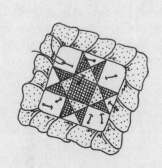

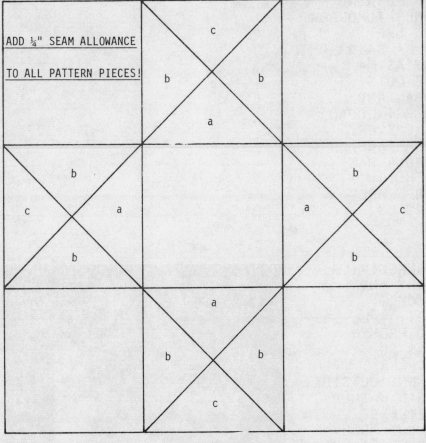

ADD ¼" SEAM ALLOWANCE
TO ALL PATTERN PIECES!

Ohio Star

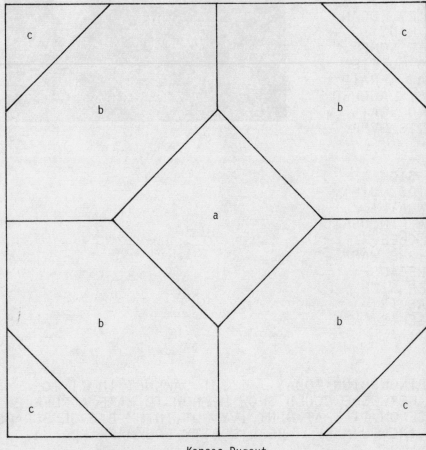

Kansas Dugout

Ma's Pincushion

Supplies -
    Fabric scraps of 3 colors. See page 38
    1 yard of 1 inch wide crocheted lace
    or 2½ X 36 inch fabric strip for ruffle
    Stuffing

Ohio Star   2 template pieces-triangle and square. Make a square of 4 triangles by piecing 1 "a" triangle to 1 "b" triangle. Piece 1 "b" triangle to one "c" triangle. Join these across the center forming a square. Repeat 3 more times. Assemble the rows, referring to the diagram. Sew the rows together forming the complete block.

Kansas Dugout   3 template pieces. Square, triangle and elongated hexagon. Piece the 4 "b" hexes to center square "a". Sew on the "c" triangles to form a square block.

Baste the crocheted lace to the outer edge of one block all the way around on the right side, keeping lace to the inside of the block, as shown. Place the second block over the first block, with right sides together, and stitch with ¼ inch seam, leaving a small opening for turning. After turning, stuff firmly with stuffing. Slip stitch opening closed.

Instead of the crocheted lace, a ruffle could be added. Cut a strip of fabric 2½ inches wide by 36 inches long. Fold in half lengthwise, with right sides out. Gather with small running stitches to fit around the pieced block and baste in place, with raw edges together, keeping the ruffle to the inside of the block. Proceed as above.

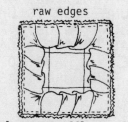

raw edges

lace or ruffle to the
inside of the block

NOVEMBER 21 PA CAME HOME THIS MORNING
WITH PRAIRIE CHICKENS FOR DINNER TOMORROW.
MA SAID WE WILL HAVE A FEAST. SHE
STARTED COOKING YESTERDAY AND PA SAID
HE COULDN'T STACK WOOD AS FAST AS MA
USED IT. WE ARE GOING TO HAVE LOTS
OF COMPANY. MR. AND MRS. LOGAN AND
CHARITY ARE COMING. MA SAYS MRS. LOGAN
MAKES THE BEST CREAM LAYER CAKE EVER.
MR. TURNER AND HARRIET AND HIRAM ARE
COMING. PA SAID MR. TURNER HAD A HAM
TO BRING. I HOPE THEY BRING THEIR
CHECKER GAME. I HAVE TO GET UP EARLY
TOMORROW TO HELP MA WITH THE ROLLS
FOR DINNER.

NOVEMBER 23 WE HAD A GOOD THANKSGIVING.
I WISH AUNT IVY AND UNCLE HENRY AND
GRAMMA AND GRANPA COULD HAVE COME.
THEN IT WOULD HAVE BEEN PERFECT. ALL
THE FOOD WAS SO GOOD. PA READ FROM
THE BIBLE A LONG TIME AND I WAS SO
HUNGRY AND I COULD SMELL FOOD. PA
AND MR. TURNER AND MR. LOGAN WENT OUTSIDE
AFTER DINNER. MA AND MRS. LOGAN WASHED
UP THE DISHES, SO I PLAYED CHECKERS
WITH HIRAM. I WOULD HAVE WON BUT MOLLY
GRABBED THE CHECKERS AND WE COULDN'T
REMEMBER WHERE TO PUT THEM. I SAT
ON PA'S LAP WHEN HE PLAYED CHECKERS
WITH MR. TURNER AND PA WON. MR. LOGAN
STARTED SINGING. HE KNOWS SO MANY
SONGS. I WISH I COULD REMEMBER SOME
OF THEM. WHEN WE WERE SINGING MUFFIE
ATE SOME OF THE CHICKEN. I WAS AFRAID
MA WOULD SMACK HER BUT SHE JUST LAUGHED
AND SAID IT WAS THANKSGIVING FOR CATS
TOO. I AM SORRY THANKSGIVING IS OVER
BUT CHRISTMAS IS COMING.

NOVEMBER 26 MA THOUGHT I WAS SICK
TODAY BECAUSE SHE SAID I WAS TOO QUIET.
BUT I DIDN'T WANT HER TO SEE WHAT I
WAS DOING. I STARTED MAKING A PINCUSHION
FOR HER FOR CHRISTMAS. MISS MCGEE
DREW ME A PATTERN FOR IT WHEN SHE WAS
HERE. ONE SIDE IS OHIO STAR BECAUSE
MA WAS BORN IN OHIO. THE OTHER SIDE
IS KANSAS DUGOUT BECAUSE KANSAS IS
OUR HOME. I HAVE SO MANY PRESENTS
TO MAKE FOR CHRISTMAS.

NOVEMBER 29 I FINISHED MA'S PINCUSHION TODAY. I PUT SAWDUST IN IT TO
MAKE IT FAT. IF AUNT IVY WAS HERE SHE COULD SHOW ME HOW TO MAKE A RUFFLE
FOR IT. I USED A PIECE OF LACE ON IT THAT AUNT IVY PUT IN MY BAG OF SCRAPS.
MA WILL BE SURPRISED. I AM GOING TO MAKE A REAL PRETTY BOOKMARK FOR PA
TO PUT IN HIS BIBLE.

PA'S BOOKMARK

Supplies -
   Muslin, broadcloth, feed sack, onasburg
   cloth, etc.
   Embroidery floss, 3 strands
   Embroidery needle

This would make a very good first project
for a little girl to try her hand. The
fabric could be tea dyed. Two layers
of muslin or broadcloth should be used
for extra body. If this is to look like
Sarah made it, the knots and threads
should show on the back.

Trace the design onto the fabric. Cut
out, leaving ½ inch seam allowance all
the way around to turn under and hem
after embroidering. A running stitch
or outline stitch may be used for the
diagonal lines. Outline stitch the hearts
and make small french knots around the
hearts. After hemming, attach a 6 inch
piece of ½ inch wide grosgrain ribbon
at the top.

This is just an extra
tiny doll for fun.
Sarah liked to wear it
pinned to her dress.

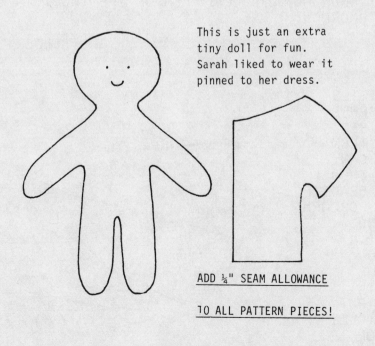

ADD ¼" SEAM ALLOWANCE

TO ALL PATTERN PIECES!

DECEMBER 5 AFTER MY STUDIES TODAY,
MA GAVE ME A PIECE OF CLOTH TO MAKE
PA'S BOOKMARK. MA DREW THE LINES ON
IT SO THEY WOULD BE STRAIGHT. I AM
GOING TO SEW IT IN RED AND GREEN FOR
CHRISTMAS. I KNOW PA WILL LIKE IT
A WHOLE LOT. I HAVE A PIECE OF RED
RIBBON TO PUT ON IT. I DON'T KNOW
WHAT TO MAKE FOR MOLLY AND MUFFIE.

DECEMBER 11 MA GAVE ME SOME CATNIP TODAY FOR MUFFIE'S PRESENT. I KNOW
MUFFIE WILL LIKE IT BECAUSE SHE WANTED TO SIT ON MY LAP WHEN I WAS TYING
IT IN A LITTLE BAG. I PUT HER OUTSIDE. IT WON'T BE A SURPRISE IF SHE
SEES IT BEFORE CHRISTMAS.

DECEMBER 17 I MADE A KITTY AND A PUPPIE FOR MOLLY TODAY. I DRAWED THEM
ALL BY MYSELF. THEY AREN'T VERY BIG BUT I DIDN'T HAVE A BIG ENUF PIECE
OF CLOTH. I SEWED SOME TOGETHER. MA SAID IT LOOKED LIKE A CRAZY QUILT.
I DON'T KNOW IF THAT MEANS IT LOOKS GOOD OR BAD. I THINK CRAZY IS BAD.
I HOPE MOLLY LIKES THEM. I EVEN SEWED FACES ON. IT SNOWED TODAY. PA
IS HUNTING AND I WISH HE WOULD COME HOME.

DECEMBER 18 PA CAME HOME WITH A DEER AND A CHRISTMAS TREE. HE SAID WE
COULDN'T BRING IT IN YET. MA SAID WE SHOULD MAKE SOME DECORATIONS FOR
IT. I TRIED TO STRING POPCORN BUT IT KEEPS BREAKING. MA SAID SHE WOULD
FINISH IT. I USED THE COOKIE CUTTER PA MADE TO DRAW LITTLE DOLLS LIKE
HANNAH. I AM GOING TO HANG THEM ON THE CHRISTMAS TREE. MUFFIE FOUND
HER PRESENT AND I WAS SO MAD. MA SAID SHE WOULD PUT IT IN A TIN SO MUFFIE
COULDN'T FIND IT.

DECEMBER 22 I FINISHED THE DOLLS. I MADE 10 OF THEM WITH DRESSES AND
ALL DIFFERENT COLOR HAIR. I DON'T KNOW HOW TO HANG THEM ON THE TREE.
PA IS GOING TO BRING THE TREE IN TOMORROW.

DECEMBER 23 LAST NIGHT MA MADE LITTLE
HEARTS AFTER I WENT TO BED. SHE SEWED
MY LITTLE DOLLS TO THEM. ALL OF THE
DOLLS ARE IN A STRING AND EACH OF THEM
HAS A HEART BETWEEN THEM. NOW WE CAN
HANG THEM ON THE TREE. MA CALLED THEM
A GARLAND. OUR CHRISTMAS TREE IS BEAUTIFUL.
THE SPICE COOKIES ARE ON IT. THE POPCORN
STRING IS REAL LONG AND GOES AROUND
AND AROUND. WE PUT MY DOLLS RIGHT
IN THE MIDDLE. MA SAID IT WAS TOO
BAD WE DIDN'T HAVE AN ANGEL FOR THE
TOP. I CUT OUT WINGS FOR ELIZABETH
AND TIED THEM ON WITH STRING. PA PUT
HER ON THE TOP OF THE TREE. BUT MOLLY
CRIED WHEN SHE SAW ELIZABETH ON TOP
OF THE TREE. I MADE HER A NEW BABY.
MUFFIE CLIMBED THE TREE AND WE COULDN'T
FIND HER.

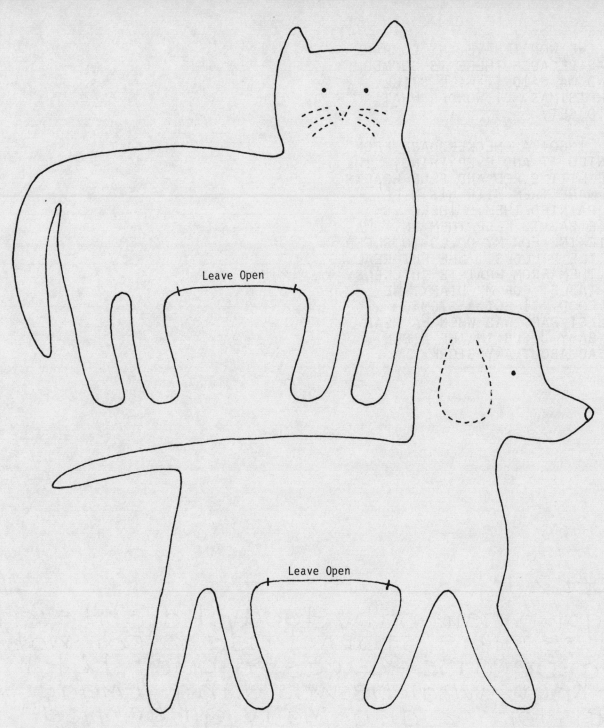

Leave Open

Leave Open

MOLLY'S TOYS

Supplies -
    Scraps of fabric, feed sack, tightly
    woven wool, etc. See page 38
    Stuffing
    Embroidery floss, 3 strands

These fabric toys need to be made from
a fairly tightly woven fabric. The all
cotton "homespun-looking" kitchen towels
that are available most everywhere would
be a good choice. They can be tea-dyed
for an old look. Any old-looking fabric
that is tightly woven would work.

ADD ¼" SEAM ALLOWANCE

TO ALL PATTERN PIECES!

Transfer patterns to template material.
Trace pattern onto wrong side of fabric,
fold fabric with right sides together.
Sew, by hand or machine, on drawn line,
leaving an opening. Turn, stuff and
slipstitch opening closed. Embroider
features with contrasting floss.

DECEMBER 24 WE WON'T HAVE ANY COMPANY
FOR CHRISTMAS BECAUSE THERE IS SO MUCH
SNOW. PA AND MA SAID IT WILL STILL
BE A GOOD CHRISTMAS. I WONDER WHAT
I AM GOING TO GET?

DECEMBER 25 I GOT A CHECKERBOARD FROM
PA. HE PAINTED IT AND EVERYTHING. THE
CHECKERS ARE LITTLE RED AND BLUE HEARTS.
UNCLE HENRY MADE THEM WITH HIS NIFE
FOR ME. PA PAINTED THEM. THERE IS
EVEN A LITTLE BAG TO KEEP THEM IN. MA
MADE ME A TICKING FOR MY DOLLS TO SLEEP
ON AND 2 LITTLE PILLOWS. SHE PUT REAL
FEATHERS IN THEM FROM PRAIRIE CHICKENS.
I GOT A NEW TABLET FOR MY DIARY. WE
ATE SO MUCH FOOD. I GOT A STOMACH
ACHE. THE BEST PART WAS WHEN PA READ
TO US ABOUT BABY JESUS IN THE BIBLE.
PA DIDN'T READ ABOUT ANY STORK.

December 29

Ma got a new baby today. I didn't even get to see the stork. I had to boil water for Ma because Pa was so busy, but I don't know what he was doing. I made supper for Me and Molly all by myself. The new baby cried and made Molly cry and Pa came out with our new brother. Pa cried too. But I didn't because I really did want a boy baby. Ma said we are going to name him Joseph. I thought he was going to be bigger. Pa let me hold him. New babies are so nice, I hope Ma has lots more of them.

Garland

Supplies
    Fabric scraps. See page 38
    Stuffing
    Embroidery floss

To make a garland 36 inches long, you will need 10 dolls and 9 hearts. These small dolls and dresses are made just like the bigger ones. The hearts can be cut from turkey red fabric or piece small scraps together for some of them. Sew hearts with the right sides together, leaving opening as shown. Turn and stuff. Slipstitch opening closed. Sew the dolls hands to the hearts at point shown on the hearts.

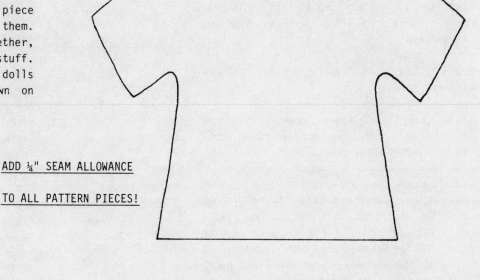

ADD ¼" SEAM ALLOWANCE

TO ALL PATTERN PIECES!

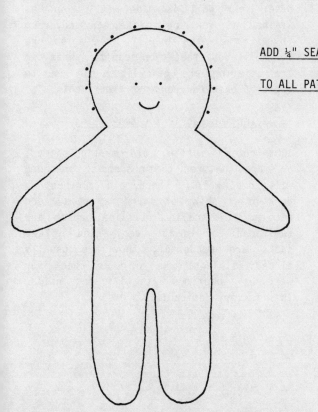

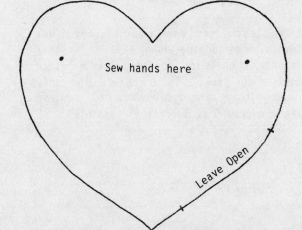

Sew hands here

Leave Open

SEWING LIKE A LITTLE GIRL

Since the price of antiques is escalating every day, the wonderful collectibles which were made in the last century have been priced out of the range of average collectors. So why not recreate them yourself? The innocent charm of a doll quilt made by a little girl 100 years ago can be yours without spending a fortune. All it takes is old or tea-dyed fabric and the ability to sew like a child, and that is the fun part! We have all trained ourselves to perfect our sewing techniques and now we can cast perfection aside and have fun! If you have a little girl to help you, so much the better. They will piece in ways you never thought of.

Some guidelines -

*Do not try to cut perfect templates. In fact, when you draw off a template don't use a ruler.

*When piecing, do not pin fabric; lay pieces together and start sewing.
Instead of taking small neat stitches, make yourself sew as fast as you can to the end.

*Don't use co-ordinating thread. Black is very good.

*Use long and short running stitches on the doll clothing and let them show. It will add to the charm.

*Don't sew in a straight line. When one of our daughters (age 12) tried some piecing, we found that her stitches were more like this / / / / /. When piecing the Flying Geese, she didn't bother to stop at the end of a seam and start over; she sewed on the first triangle and went right on to the second.

*She also pieced some on the wrong side, turned some upside down, and in general taught us quite a lot about how a little girl might sew. To a child, the only reason they are sewing is to achieve the end result as quickly as possible.

Be sure to add a name and date on your finished project.

If you sign SARAH 1883, sign your name and the year below. We do not condone making antiques; we are creating reproductions.

MAKING OLD FABRIC

Because this book recreates 100 year old dolls, clothing and accessories, all of the fabric used must look old. In only a few cases were we fortunate enough to have truly old fabric to work with. Therefore, by various means and experimentation, we made our own "old" fabric. Experimentation doesn't really tell it all. Our families waited patiently for "Mom's soup", only to find out that it was fabric bubbling happily in the stock pot on the back burner. What looked like a terminal old rag was tossed out with the trash several times before becoming a doll. Shirts have disappeared almost off of our families backs to be made into "old" doll dresses. A friend of one of our daughters vowed not to return until the book was finished, because of his preference for shirts with a definate "homespun" look. All of this is merely leading up to the fact that only by experimenting will you achieve the "old" fabric look that you desire. There are no hard and fast rules. If, after your doll is made, it is not as stained as you would like, try covering it with wet tea bags. There's no one to tell you that you can't. What we are offering are guidelines for you to use as a base for your own experiments.

1. Selecting fabric for tea-dyeing

100% cotton muslin, old muslin sheets, or more textured cloth such as onasburg will dye well. Check old clothes; a dark print shirt or skirt may have faded nicely. Old calico curtains, which are sun-faded, would be very good. Feed sacks are wonderful; they are usually already stained. Be sure to check for writing; sometimes it will be inside. This is very desirable.

When selecting new fabric for tea-dyeing, look for light backgrounds or dark prints with white designs. Plaids and checks are also good. Just remember, there needs to be some white or very light space for the tea-dyeing to be effective. Use only small cuts of fabric, ½ yard or less. This will make rinsing much easier. Invariably the tea bags will break, so there will be tea leaves to rinse off.

Try to dye your fabric in batches of the same color family. It is preferable to start with light backgrounds and end with darks in case the colors run.

2. Making "old" fabric

We made our own "old" fabric by various means. The easiest method, especially for small amounts, is tea-dying. This is done several ways. It is most effective if done in a large pot on the stove. Bring water to boil (1/2 to 2/3 pot full) add 10-20 tea bags depending on the size of pot and the depth of color desired. Cover the pot to steep the tea. In about 5 minutes, add fabric. Do not try to cram the pot full. All fabric should be covered by the dye bath, leaving sufficient room to stir the fabric. Cover pot and let simmer. Stir fabric frequently, checking for color. Keep in mind that the fabric will dry lighter. The first dye bath should take only 30 minutes to 1 hour. Remove fabric, squeezing excess dye out and add more fabric to the dye bath and continue simmering. Rinse dyed fabric in cold water. Wring and dry in dryer. Two or three batches can be dyed with the same tea. Usually by the third batch, we turn off the stove and leave the fabric overnight.

For primarily white or light backgrounds, a no cook method can be used. In a large mixing bowl or pot, pour boiling water over 10-12 tea bags. Cover for a short time. Add fabric so all of it is covered with tea water. Stir occasionally and check for color. Rinse as above. Dry.

For very stained looking fabric

Option 1: Use loose tea leaves. Soak fabric in water and tea leaves as above. Remove from water, squeezing lightly allowing the tea leaves to remain on the fabric. Bunch fabric onto a cookie sheet; do not smooth out. Place in a 300 degree oven. Check frequently, every 5 minutes or so; the fabric will start smoking as it dries, and stains will be created. Some of the stains may rinse out, but many will remain. Leave fabric in the oven about 15-20 minutes. Rinse and dry.

Option 2: Wet fabric thoroughly. Lay out flat and apply tea leaves or coffee grounds all over the surface of the fabric. Fold to contain the tea or coffee and continue folding to create a bundle. Allow to dry completely. Rinse well to remove tea or coffee. Dry.

One word of warning. Tea-dye will wash out with detergents. If you ever plan to wash the fabric that you have dyed, it is best to hand wash in cold water with very mild soap. If you wish to set the dye in a fabric that will be washed often, you can use ½ cup of vinegar in a gallon of water. Soak the fabric in this mixture for a few minutes. Rinse and dry.

HOW TO SEW THE DOLLS

Supplies
   Muslin, feed sack, onasburg cloth, broadcloth, etc. See page 38
   Black or brown solids for shoes
   Various fabric scraps for clothing. See page
   Old knee sock for cap for boy doll
   Stuffing
   Embroidery floss
   Embroidery needles
   Buttons for eyes, if desired

Dolls (without separate legs)

Transfer patterns to template material. Trace around the template on the wrong side of fabric. Fold fabric with the right sides together and pin to hold it in place. Stitch the entire outline either by hand or machine. Cut out, leaving ¼ inch beyond the stitched seam.

Clip corners of neck, underarms and between legs. Cut a 2 inch opening along the center back fabric, taking care not to cut through both layers. Turn doll through this cut. Stuff firmly. Slipstitch opening closed. Run a line of stitches just above the legs, mushing the stuffing out of the way as you stitch. This will enable your doll to sit. Embroider hair and features as desired. See page   .

These dolls can have shoes added to them, without making seperate legs, if you wish. Sew a 3" X 17" piece of black or brown fabric to the lower edge of the body fabric. Fold with right sides together and proceed as described above, tracing around the template for shoes onto dark fabric.

Dolls (with separate legs)

Transfer patterns to template material
For legs with colored shoes, sew a 3 X 12 inch strip of black or brown to a 4 X 12 strip of body fabric. On wrong side of fabric, (just use half of it) trace on 2 sets of legs and shoes, connecting legs and shoes at seam line. Fold fabric with right sides together, pin to hold in place. Stitch along drawn line leaving top edge open. Cut out leaving ¼ inch seam allowance and clip curves. Turn and stuff firmly, leaving ¼ inch at top edge unstuffed. For the feet to face forward, the seam lines will be in the center of the front and back. Baste top edge closed.

Trace around body template on the wrong side of fabric. Fold the fabric with right sides together and pin to hold in place. Stitch the outline either by hand or machine, leaving the lower edge open. Cut out, leaving a ¼ inch seam allowance. Clip curves and corners. Turn. Turn under fabric ¼ inch on lower edge of body and baste. Stuff firmly. Insert stuffed legs in lower edge opening and pin in place. Stitch. Embroider hair and features as desired.

Clothing

Printing limitations have made it necessary to draw only half of the clothing (shown with a center fold in the drawing). These should be converted to a full template by repeating the other half on your template material. This will avoid confusion.

Draw around the dress template onto the wrong side of fabric. Fold the fabric with right sides together. Pin to hold in place. Sew shoulder seams and underarm and side seams. Clip underarm seams. Turn. Hem the lower edge. Hem arm and neck holes with running stitches. Do not knot thread at the end. Leave 3-4 inches of thread hanging. Dress doll. Rethread the needle with the hanging thread. Draw up thread to gather excess fabric at each arm and around the neck. Secure thread with a knot and cut off.

Dress with set-in sleeves

Sew only shoulder seams. Cut out 2 sleeves and gather along the line shown. With right sides together, sew sleeves to dress matching notches. Sew under arm seam and dress side seam all at once. Turn under raw edge of sleeve and hem. Hem the lower edge of dress. This is a more fitted sleeve and does not need the excess fabric gathered at the wrist. Hem neckline as above and gather after dressing the doll.

Dress with gathered skirt

Cut one bodice with center front on fold.
Cut 2 bodice allowing 3/8 inch extra at center (not on fold) for backs.
Sew front to two backs at shoulder seams and underarms. Clip underarms and turn. For set-in sleeves, see instructions above. Gather skirt on one long side, with small running stitches, to fit lower edge of bodice. Sew with right sides together, matching center of skirt to center front of bodice. Sew a ¼ inch seam allowance from hem line to 1 inch below waist at center back. Turn under neckline, lower edge of sleeve and lower edge of skirt ¼ inch and hem.
Place a small snap at neck line and waist line at back of dress.

Pantaloons for girl

Trace onto wrong side of the fabric. Fold fabric, with the right sides together and pin to hold in place. Sew outer and inner leg seams. Cut out. Hem the lower edge of the leg holes. Hem waist but do not knot thread at the end. Leaving the needle threaded, put the pants on the doll and draw up thread to fit doll. Tie off thread.

Trousers for boy

Follow instructions for the girls pants, except hem waistband without gathering. Cut 2 strips of fabric, 1" X 8½", to make suspenders. Press raw edges toward the center and fold in half lengthwise to make a strip about ¼ inch wide. Stitch.

Cut in half to make 2 suspenders. Tack suspenders in front at waistband. Cross strips in back and tack to trousers waistband.

Cap for boy

For the largest doll, an adult size knee length sock will make 2 or 3 caps. Measuring from the top edge of the sock, cut off 5 inches. At the cut edge, tie string or strong thread about ½ inch from the cut edge. Tie string as tightly as possible. Turn cap so string is inside. Pull over dolls head and fold lower edge up about ½ inch. Fold up again. If you wish the fold could be stitched to hold it in place. We have not found it to be necessary, nor have we had a problem with cut edges unraveling.

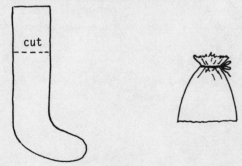

A child size sock will fit the medium doll, or mittens can be used. We all seem to have an ample supply of unmatched mittens.

Pinafore.

Trace onto the wrong side of the fabric. Fold the fabric with right sides together. Pin to hold in place. Sew shoulder and side seams. Cut out leaving ¼ inch seam allowance. Hem neckline, arm holes and the lower edge.

Apron

Cut a piece of fabric 3½ X 6 inches. Hem under 3 sides leaving one 6 inch side unhemmed. Gather this side to 3 inches wide. Cut a strip of fabric 1 X 17 inches.

Press raw edges toward center and fold in half lengthwise to make a strip about ¼ inch wide. Match the center of the apron to the center of this strip and pin. With the gathered edge of the apron inside the folded edges of the strip, sew along the folds the entire length. Tie apron directly under the doll's arms.

This apron fits all the dolls except Elizabeth. Her apron is 2¼ X 4.

Slip

A knitted slip for any of the dolls may be made by using a man's old undershirt and the pinafore pattern. (If your family is like ours, it won't even be necessary to tea dye the undershirt.)

Any of the clothing can be enhanced by small amounts of crocheted lace, tatting, old lace, patches, pockets, etc.

Bandana

Cut triangle of fabric from pattern, noting the fold line on the pattern. Hem all edges. Tie the base of the triangle (longest edge) around neck of doll. The point of the triangle should come over the top of her head. Instead of hemming, the bandana edges may be fringed.

Amish Dolls

All of these dolls are easily made into Amish dolls. Amish dolls had no facial features or hair. They always wore black bonnets and solid dark colored clothing.

Bonnet

Using a doll template, draw around the head shape only, onto plain black fabric. Cut out leaving ¼ inch seam allowance. This is the bonnet back. For the brim, use the correct size from the chart. This is the size to cut and includes seam allowance. Fold cut strip in half lengthwise, right sides together. Stitch both short ends according to the diagram:

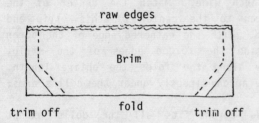

Trim the triangle that has been created. Turn right sides out and iron. Hem lower edge of bonnet back ¼ inch. Pin center of the brim to the top center of bonnet back. Stitch brim to the bonnet back sewing along drawn line. Cut a 24 inch strip of black fabric 3/4 inch wide. (For Elizabeth this strip needs to be only 17 X 3/4 inches.) Fold the strip twice to make a long piece ¼ inch wide. Iron. With the raw edge of the strip against the lower edge of the bonnet, match the centers of the strip and bonnet back. Pin along bonnet back and sides. Sew the entire length of the strip by hand or machine.

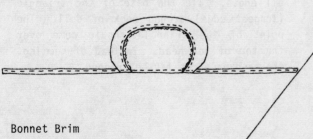

Bonnet Brim

Hannah 11 X 4 inches
Josephine 6 5/8 X 1½ inches
Elizabeth 5 5/8 X 1½
Pearl 6 5/8 X 1½ inches
Effie 8¼ X 2 inches

ADD ¼" SEAM ALLOWANCE

TO ALL PATTERN PIECES!

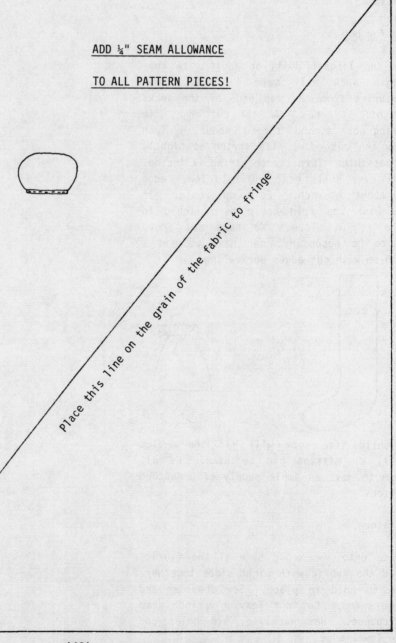

Place this line on the grain of the fabric to fringe

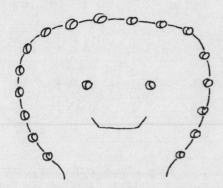

Eyes are small french knots. Mouth is
stitched with black or red floss. One
long and two short stitches. See drawing.

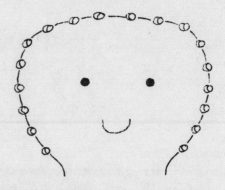

Features are drawn on with an extra fine
point, permanent, felt tip pen. Try it
on a scrap of fabric first.

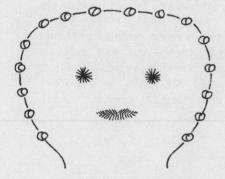

Eyes are stitched, using single strand
floss. This is very effective in white
on a black doll. Satin stitched lips
with black or red floss. They don't have
to be filled in completely.

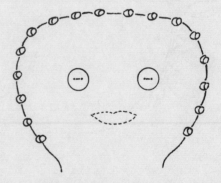

Eyes are small black or white buttons.
These must be sewn on before stuffing.
Mouth is outline stitched in black or
red floss.

The mouth can also be a straight line
of short stitches:-------

When putting the hair and facial features
on the dolls, it should look spontaneous!
Do not mark the placement, judge it by
eye-balling. All of the hair and faces
can be stitched before or after stuffing.
When you are choosing floss for these,
do not overlook some of the less obvious
colors such as dirty golds, rusts, browns,
etc. You can also use threads other than
floss. We have used carpet thread, black
string, and regular cotton sewing thread.

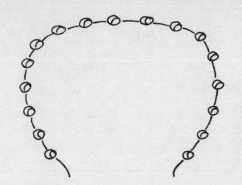
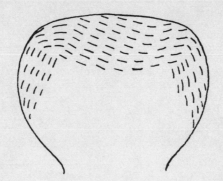
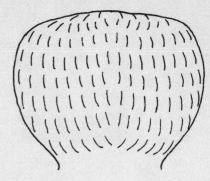

Traditional hair:
French knots are done on the face side, very close to the seam, about 3/8" apart. (On the small doll they should be about 1/4" apart.) Use a very long thread with 6 strands of floss (3 strands on small doll). Pop the knot through from the back and continue making french knots until all are done. Do not cut the thread after each knot.

Pretty hair:
Use a very long thread with 1 or 2 strands of floss or thread. Stitch as shown, all over the head. See drawing.

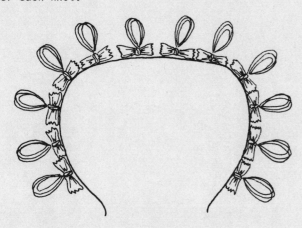

Rag curls:
These are loops of floss tied with rags. The rags are torn 1/4" wide from stained muslin. These are done on the face side close to the seam, about 5/8" apart. Use a very long thread with 6 strands of floss. Bring needle out and back in at the same spot, leaving a loop of floss about 1/2" long. Tie this loop before starting the next loop. Continue until all the loops are made.

Braids:
These are done close to the seam on the face side. Use a single strand of cotton speed crosheen. Go around the head leaving 3 strands in each hole. See drawing. Leave the strands about 2" long. Clip apart as shown. Braid each group of 3 about 1". Tie with floss and trim to about 1 1/2".

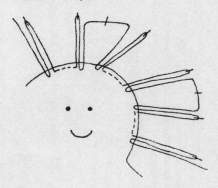

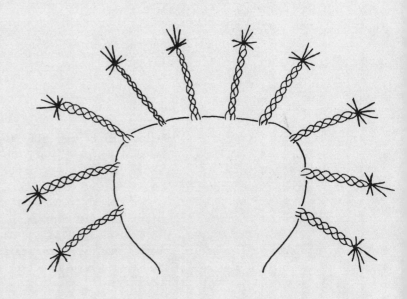

Linda Brannock lives in Independence, Missouri with her husband, Bob, and Muffy the cat. She has a daughter and grandson in California and a daughter and grandson in Florida and is awaiting the arrival of new grandchildren this fall from each state. She also has a son graduating from college this year. She is President of the Quilter's Guild of Greater Kansas City and an active member of Kaw Valley Quilter's Guild. She has taught quilting for eight years.

Linda is the co-author of HEARTS for American Country Homes and the author of numerous quilt patterns, including Star of Hearts.

Linda loves hearts, stars, houses, antiques, chocolate, her cat, and anything blue.

Joan Vibert lives in Leawood, Kansas with her husband, Jim, four children, Holly the dog, and Angel the cat. Between Joan and Jim, they have seven children; six teenagers and a twenty-two year old. If that isn't enough, she owns and operates Evening Star Farm and teaches workshops across the country. She is an active member of the Quilter's Guild of Greater Kansas City and Kaw Valley Quilter's Guild.

Joan is a prolific stenciler and the author of PRAIRIE PATTERNS, COUNTRY PATTERNS and numerous quilt patterns.

Joan loves cats, sailing, antiques, books, bare-feet, quilts, and sunshine.

Linda and Joan have a friendship that has endured living 25 miles apart. Working on this book has meant hours of driving for Linda, gasoline bills for Bob, quick lunches for Joan to think up, and hours of entertainment for Jim, who offices from home and always needed the word processor.

With the completion of this book, Linda and Joan are still friends and have homes and families intact. They are planning a sequel as Sarah Jane grows up.

We dedicate this book to our sons, Bob, Scott and Bear, who never knew the pleasures of being little girls.

A giant "Thank You" to Jim Vibert, our photographer, (and Joan's husband). It took a great amount of patience on Jim's part and several week-ends in the darkroom, when he could have been working on his sailboat!